Drawing
from the
Heart

My Heart Has a Window!, Susan-Marie Beauchemin

Drawing *from the* Heart

A SEVEN-WEEK PROGRAM TO HEAL EMOTIONAL PAIN AND LOSS THROUGH EXPRESSIVE ART

Barbara Ganim

Quest Books

Theosophical Publishing House

Wheaton, Illinois ♦ Chennai (Madras), India

The Theosophical Society acknowledges with gratitude the generous support of the Kern Foundation for the publication of this book.

First Quest Edition 2004

> The Theosophical Publishing House
> P. O. Box 270
> Wheaton, IL 60189-0270

Cover and text design and typesetting by Beth Hansen-Winter

Library of Congress Cataloging-in-Publication Data

Ganim, Barbara.
Drawing from the heart: a seven-week program to heal emotional pain and loss through expressive art / Barbara Ganim.
     p. cm.
ISBN 0-8356-0832-8
1. Art therapy.   2. Drawing—Therapeutic use.   3. Drawing—Psychological aspects.   4. Healing.   5. Self-help techniques.   I. Title.

RC489.A7G363 2004
616.89'1656—dc22
                                                            2003064678

5   4   3   2   1   *   04   05   06   07   08   09   10

Printed in Hong Kong through Global Interprint, Santa Rosa, California

Dedication

To my parents,
ALICE AND LAWRENCE GANIM

Their love was from the heart

Contents

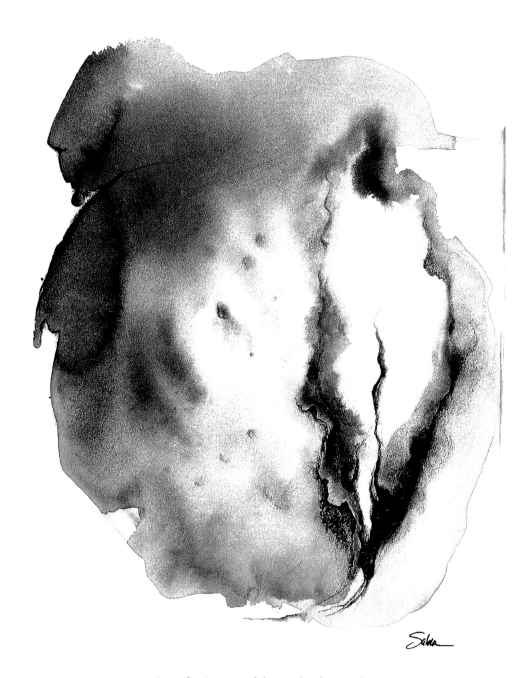

View of Existence of the Soul, Sabra Park

Acknowledgments

My first thank-you must go to the members of my two Drawing from the Heart support groups at Saint Paul's Episcopal Church in Wickford, Rhode Island. Without your dedication and enthusiasm for this work and your willingness to share your drawings and healing experiences, this book could never have been written. You all taught me more than you know.

A special thank-you to the Reverend Mary Canavan: you made this all possible by opening the church to the groups, giving us the space to meet, and the support and encouragement to continue.

I also want to thank Margaret Webb, Saint Paul's pastoral coordinator, for soliciting group members and giving me valuable guidance and insight.

My deepest gratitude to my dearest friend Lili Costa: you are, as Stephen King would say, my "Ideal Reader." Your inspiration, your wisdom, and honest reactions as the book unfolded kept me focused,

grounded, and encouraged. Your first-cut editing was invaluable.

To Susan Fox, my long-time friend, colleague, and play buddy: thank you for always listening and for your wonderful ideas. And thank you for cofacilitating several of the group sessions. It was a great experience for all of us.

A heartfelt thank-you to my agent, Julie Hill, for believing in me, loving the book, and getting behind it when it was no more than a glimmer of an idea.

My appreciation also goes to Michael Fusaro, photographer at East Greenwich Photo in East Greenwich, Rhode Island, for your expert photographic skills and careful handling of the artwork for this book.

And finally I must thank Sharron Dorr, Publishing Manager at Quest Books for your support of this project, your creative contribution to the title, and teaching me without realizing it the importance of "less is more."

Figure 1: *Anger,* by Shawn Crawford

"Before I began this drawing, I could feel the anger in the pit of my stomach. It felt like a tightly wound coil, because I had been trying so hard to hold it in for so many years. When I drew what that coil felt like, for the first time the tightness in my stomach was gone."

Drawing from the Heart

Anger was nothing new for Shawn Crawford. It had been with her since childhood. Now in her mid-forties, Shawn was tired of feeling it, tired of the separation it created between herself and others. When Shawn joined one of the seven-week Drawing from the Heart support groups I ran as a testing ground for this book, she told the group she had tried for years to deal with her anger through traditional talk therapy, but regardless of how much she talked about it, it wouldn't go away. To make matters worse, talking about it kept bringing up the pain all over again. She wasn't an artist, she said—at least *she* didn't think so—but she liked the idea of drawing to express emotional pain, especially drawing from her heart instead of talking from her mind, which seemed only to aggravate her feelings of anger.

After Shawn did her first drawing in group (fig. 1), she could hardly believe that drawing a bunch of circles on paper could release the anger that had gripped her insides for so long like a tightly wound steel coil. When the other participants finished their drawings, they were also surprised at how much better they felt—their pain had diminished as well. "Is it healed?" one of them asked. "Is it that simple?" someone else questioned. "Is it gone forever?"

I told them they were feeling better because drawing releases the blocked energy a painful emotion creates in the body—that part *is* simple. But their pain wasn't gone forever and it wasn't yet healed. This first drawing was just the beginning of a powerful process called Expressive Art that would, over the course of

this seven-week program, help them transform and heal their pain. This was not to imply that they would never feel pain again, but at least they would not feel *this* pain again.

Expressing how a painful emotion feels as an image on paper or through any art form is just the beginning of healing with expressive art. The final stage of healing cannot take place until we change our relationship to a difficult or painful event by changing the way we react to it. That's what my group members still needed to do.

The process of change or transformation in expressive art involves asking your heart, not your mind, for a less stressful, more positive way to respond to a painful experience. Your heart will answer your request in images, not words, because imagery, as split-brain research of the 1980s proved, is the inner language of the body-mind. More about that later.

There's a saying: Insanity is doing the same thing over again in exactly the same way, yet expecting different results. This theory applies to healing as well. If you react to your pain in the same old way, yet expect yourself to heal, it won't happen. You'll be stuck in your pain, unable to move past it, unable to heal it.

When I led my group through a transformational exercise to draw a heart-inspired symbol representing a more peaceful way to react to their painful situations, Shawn was the first to talk about her drawing (fig. 2). "My image of pain has been replaced by this soft pink heart. This drawing tells me that I can have compassion for those who have hurt me. The border around the heart represents a boundary. If I set boundaries—something I haven't done before—the people who hurt me can no longer do it. That puts me in control."

Each group member received equally insightful messages from their heart symbols. Their drawings showed them how to go through their pain without creating more pain. Their heart drawings also revealed how they could learn from their painful experiences and grow stronger because of it. We all feel beaten down by our pain, but it doesn't have to be that way. Emotional pain is a great teacher if we allow ourselves to heed the lessons. This is the beginning of the recovery process.

Drawing Gives Voice to the Heart

Finding a less stressful way to react to a painful experience rarely presents itself through the mind, because our judgments and fears always intervene. Only the voice of the heart, conveyed through our inner language of imagery, can offer a more loving and peaceful way to respond to that painful experience.

When you draw an image of how an emotion feels inside your body, you release the stress-producing hold that emotion has, not only on your body, but your mind and spirit as well. When you draw an image from the heart, you receive a message that tells you how to heal your most painful emotions and deepest wounds.

The heart is the voice of wisdom. Drawing is the conduit through which that voice can speak. Your heart, if you let it, will guide you through every painful experience or devastating event with insight, compassion, and a perspective the mind cannot fathom. Seeing your pain through the window of the heart opens pathways you never imagined.

This seven-step healing program can help you express and transform your own feelings of emotional pain and loss. To make the program easier to follow, I have divided the book into two parts. Part One consists of six chapters that tell you all about the program—how it works and why. Part Two contains exercises for each of the seven healing steps.

Figure 2: *Compassion*, a transformational heart drawing by Shawn Crawford

"This drawing told me that I could open my heart with compassion to those who had hurt me, but still protect myself by establishing personal boundaries—something I hadn't done before."

Figure 3: *Heart Symbol of Pain*, by M. E. Madsen

PART ONE

Everything You Need to Know about This Seven-Step Healing Program

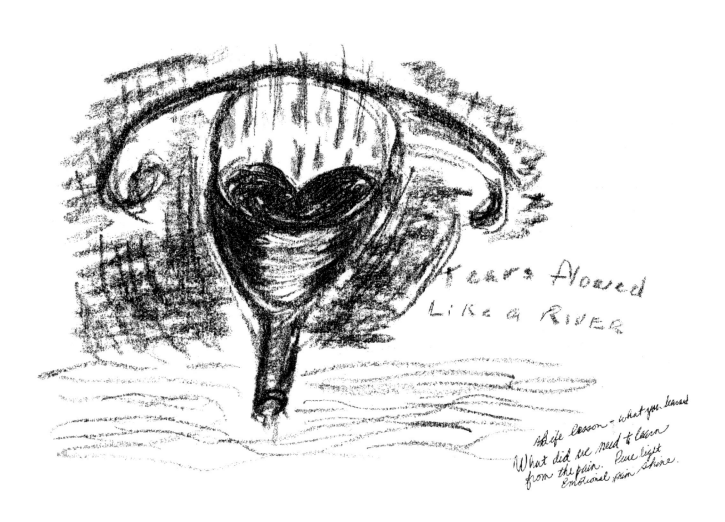

Figure 4: *Tears Flowed Like a River,* by Phyllis Seelen

"Pain isn't a bad thing. I learned that a long time ago from a hymn that goes like this: 'Joy and pain come down entwined.' When I did this drawing, I saw the womb form as a funnel through which my tears could flow like a river, because tears are a part of life. This drawing is a reminder to myself that life will always be entwined with pain—you can't separate them."

Why Talking about Our Pain Can Make Us Feel Worse

During the introductory meeting of my first Drawing from the Heart support group, one of our members, Phyllis Seelen, made a poignant comment that we all needed to hear as she spoke about her first drawing (fig. 4): "Life will always be entwined with pain—you can't separate them." Phyllis was right. Painful, life-changing experiences happen to us all sooner or later; we can't avoid them. When they happen, most people do their best to deal with the pain by expressing it in the only way they know how—talking about it. But talking about pain often makes us feel even worse, because our words are frequently steeped in judgment, blame, and shame, which tend to ignite anger and rage or apathy and depression. Consequently, talking about emotional pain may accomplish only one thing: embedding the pain even deeper into our conscious awareness, making the healing process more difficult.

That doesn't mean talking can't help—it can, especially when it's done under the supervision of a skilled therapist. Yet in spite of a therapist's best efforts, our words often pull us deeper into an emotional funk, because few of us can edit out our judgmental words when we begin talking about a painful experience. Author James Pennebaker points out in his book *Opening Up: The Healing Power of Expressing Emotions* (Guilford Press,

1997), that people often stop talking about their feelings at precisely the time when they need it most—usually about three months after a painful experience has occurred—because it hurts too much to keep going over the same situation or issue. The backlash to this is that the people they have been talking to, like friends and family members, mistakenly think they are over it. But the fact is, they are not.

Without support and encouragement to keep talking about our feelings, most of us just push them down and bury them beneath layers of distracting daily events, hoping time will do its healing magic. Time doesn't heal and healing isn't magic. Left unattended, our buried wounds fester and grow until

Figure 5: *Powerlessness*, by a former client, shows how a simple drawing can express a complex emotional reaction.

another painful experience comes along, exposing all those unhealed wounds that time did not repair.

Expressive Art Is a Powerful Nonverbal Way to Express and Release Your Pain

Emotional pain and loss, if left unexpressed and unreleased, can unravel the fabric of our lives. What then are the alternatives if talking about our pain can make it hurt even more? Expressive art is now considered the most effective nonverbal way to express and release the feelings a painful emotion can produce. When we use art to express our pain, we are accessing that pain through the body-mind's inner language of imagery instead of using words.

Unlike words, our imagistic language is nonjudgmental. When a painful emotion is expressed as an image representing how our body reacts to that emotion, we avoid the negative interpretation our words often impose. A graphic image of an emotion allows us to see the colors and shapes that describe how that emotion feels inside our bodies. Expressing an emotion through color and form rather than words gives us insight into the nature of our feelings and their impact on our body, mind, and spirit. Seeing an image of what an emotion feels like brings us out of the darkness of judgment into the light of understanding where we can see the lessons our emotions can teach. These lessons can help us transform a painful emotional reaction into a positive life experience.

I decided to use drawing as the primary method of artistic expression for this book because drawing requires little in the way of materials—just chalk or oil pastels, colored markers or crayons, a sketch pad or a drawing journal, and you're ready to go. The

Figure 6: Drawing by former client expressing feelings of sadness over the death of a close friend.

space needed to do the work can be as simple as an easy chair or a porch swing. The skill involved in doing the drawing exercises presented in this book requires nothing more than the ability to hold a crayon or pastel in your hand and move it across the surface of the paper.

You Don't Have to Be an Artist

Anyone, even those without the slightest trace of artistic ability, can use this program to draw their pain. If you can make simple marks or shapes on paper that in some way represent what a painful emotion feels like, then you can use drawing to express and heal that pain.

A client I worked with several years ago was afraid, when she first came to see me, that her lack of drawing ability would prevent her from expressing her feelings about the death of a close friend. As soon as she began to draw (fig. 6), her fear disappeared. Just a few broad strokes and a small stick figure at the bottom was all she needed to fully express the feeling of sadness that had been pressing down on her for weeks like a heavy weight—a feeling she had been unable to describe in words.

Figure 7: Drawing by former client expressing the frustration she felt when dealing with her rebellious teenage daughter.

Drawing Releases Emotional Pain from the Body

Emotional pain causes physical pain, which acts as a signal to let us know when something is amiss. When we're in pain, it can be hard to pay attention to the source of that pain, especially when all we want to do is ignore it. Unlike talking, which can aggravate emotional pain, drawing that pain releases it from your body. However, releasing your pain does not solve or resolve the situation that provoked it; it simply enables you to feel physically more comfortable, so that you can concentrate on working and ultimately healing at a deep level.

Over the years, I've seen many clients learn to cope with situations that previously left them feeling like helpless victims of their emotional reactions. One such client was at wits' end after struggling for nearly a year with almost daily verbal battles between herself and her rebellious teenage daughter. By the time she came to see me, she was ready to send her daughter to boarding school—a decision she knew she would later regret.

During our first session, I showed her how to use drawing to express her feelings (fig. 7) and transform her hasty emotional reactions into more positive and constructive responses. When I saw her a week later, she looked like a totally different person. The slump in her shoulders and the tightness in her face were gone. Elated, she told me that every time she had come to blows with her daughter during the past week, she had just grabbed her sketch pad and took a

CHAPTER ONE

Figure 8: *A Flood of Tears*, by Barbara Ganim

"For nearly four years after my father's death I was unable to grieve, because I was preoccupied with my mother's Alzheimer's disease. That pain finally came out in this drawing three years ago, and the relief I felt was liberating."

few minutes alone to draw what she was feeling. "It made all the difference," she said. "Instead of reacting rashly and emotionally, I was able to deal with the situation calmly and rationally. Now my daughter and I are actually talking instead of screaming at each other. I can't believe the change in both of us."

Whenever I begin writing a new book, I like to run workshops or support groups based on the concept of the book. These groups give me an opportunity to put my ideas into practice. While writing this book, I offered two seven-week Drawing from the Heart support groups based on seven healing steps. Each group met once a week for two hours. I guided them through drawing exercises that helped them work through every phase of the drawing-from-the-heart process. After completing the program, group members graciously allowed me to share their healing stories and the drawings they produced. These will not only help you see how others have used drawing to express and heal their pain, they will also serve as examples of how to do the exercises in this book.

In addition to drawings produced by group members, I have included some drawings and stories given to me by present and former graduate students at Salve Regina University, where I teach expressive art. In some instances, to show specific examples, I use drawings by former clients and workshop participants. In each case, I have permission to use their artwork and experiences. However, a few of the artists prefer to remain anonymous. In those cases I use a pseudonym or refer to them as "former clients."

As I began writing about emotional pain and the suffering it can bring, I realized that I was also ready to tackle my own emotional demons. Therefore, a few of my drawings are also included in this book.

This Book Is for Anyone Going through a Painful Experience

Whether you are struggling with the death of a loved one, job loss or looming retirement, aging parents, personal illness, or the painful twists and turns in relationships with friends or family, you know how sad and even devastating these experiences can be. While you may desperately want to ignore what's happening in your life, unresolved emotional pain will express itself sooner or later through illness and disease, or it will reemerge during future life-altering events—magnified by months or years of neglect.

Figure 9: *Spinning off to a New Level of Awareness,* by Kina King

"This drawing was such a breakthrough! [It came] after just four weeks of using drawing to express the anger and pain I was feeling about certain people and things in my life that I wanted to change but couldn't. When I did this drawing, I suddenly realized that I had spun off and evolved to a new level of awareness—a place where for the first time I felt unaffected by the thoughts and behaviors of others."

How Drawing from the Heart Can Change Your Life

When we take the time to move past our pain, we are transformed to a new level of thinking and feeling that screens out the old, destructive thoughts that kept us attached to the opinions and actions of others. That movement is possible only when we express the pain and release it. Drawing enables us to do that. Once the pain is released, we can focus on changing ourselves instead of trying so hard to change others as Kina King, one of my group members, happily discovered (fig. 9). For Kina, this new way of thinking brought about a feeling of freedom that changed everything.

Another example of the kind of change that can occur when we change ourselves happened when one of my graduate students, artist Diana Boehnert, used expressive art to explore and heal a painful issue from her past (fig. 10). Like Kina King, with the help of her drawings, Diana started to see herself in a way that allowed her to focus on changing herself instead of trying to change others. She shared the impact of this with the class. "When I began to change myself, it influenced everyone around me. It was miraculous," she said. "My family started acting differently toward me, because I was acting differently toward them. Not a word needed to be exchanged. It just happened. I would never have believed six weeks ago that my life could change so drastically just by expressing all the painful, negative thoughts and emotions I'd been holding onto for so many years. My recent issue has been resolved, and through what seems like magic, my relationships have taken a positive turn."

Expressive art isn't magic, but it will help you heal your pain if you stay with it as Diana did. If you allow

Figure 10: *The Heart Speaks,* by Diana Boehnert
(For a color image of this picture, see page 37.)

"My drawing says: 'I am strong and sturdy. I can hold a lot of pain.' The black and blue marks and areas are dense, but they are around the edges. They are broken with deep gashes on the sides, but they don't go all the way through. There is a brighter orange on my lower left—where the dark spot was. The center has less black and blue with some light shining through. I still feel sad, but I know I can hold it together. The pain is lifting from my body."

yourself to ride the ups and downs of your emotions as they come out through your drawings, you will also experience that sense of wonder and relief as your

Figure 11: *The Other Side of the Corner: A Life of Pain,* **by Jan**
(The paper flap at the bottom turned to the left shows a woman looking back on her pain.)

pent-up emotions are transformed through the power of expressive art.

Healing Can Be Just around the Corner

Jan was in my second Drawing from the Heart group. Three weeks into the program, she came in with a drawing she did for a homework assignment. As she began to talk about it, we all noticed a new lightness in her face and demeanor. She explained her transformation. "When emotional pain has been with you for a long time," she said, "it's hard to believe that you can feel differently. But then, while doing this drawing, I imagined myself on a corner. On one side of the corner was my pain, and on the other side of the corner was a life free of pain. That's when it hit me—just because I can't see a pain-free life right now doesn't mean it doesn't exist. I just need to go around the corner to see it—to be willing

6-17-02
The other side of the corner

Figure 12: *The Other Side of the Corner: A Life without Pain,* **by** Jan
(The paper flap at the bottom turned to the right shows a woman looking toward a life free of pain.)

to move away from my pain." On the bottom of her drawing, Jan had added a little flap of paper. When turned to the left (fig. 11), it depicted a woman in despair, because she was looking back in the direction of her pain. When turned to the right (fig. 12), it showed the same woman filled with hope as she looked around the corner toward a life without pain. Jan said, "This was the first time I actually believed that I could have a life without pain, and that was a big awakening."

Seeing the progress others make as they work through their painful issues and begin to heal is one of the best things about being part of a support group. My intention in sharing the artwork and healing stories of my group members is to give you that same opportunity to witness their struggles as well as their accomplishments. When others heal, it gives hope to those still trapped in the pain of their experiences, wondering if that pain will ever go away. It will, but only if it's expressed.

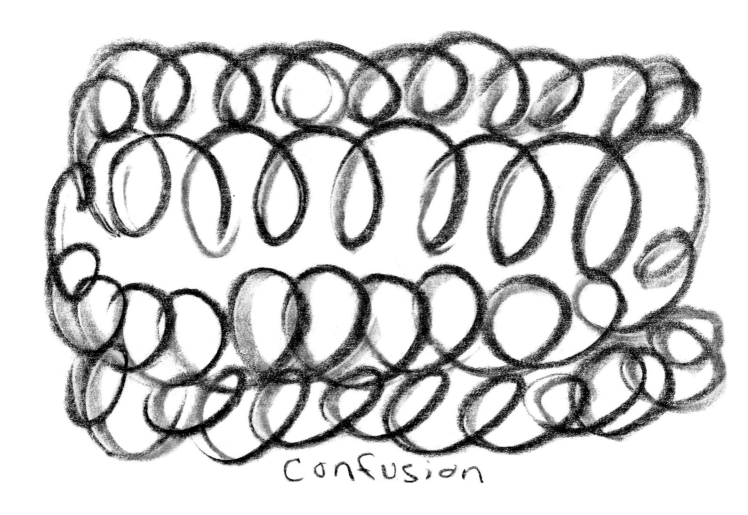

Figure 13: *Confusion,* drawing by former client

Why a Picture Is Worth a Thousand Words

Several years ago a client I'll call Rachel was in the throes of divorce when she first came to see me. She and her husband were separated, but she couldn't bring herself to sign the final divorce documents. Her opening plea to me was, "I'm so confused. I don't know what I'm feeling." Traditional talk therapy was not helping her sort out her conflicted feelings. During our first session, Rachel nervously told me that she couldn't draw. I allayed her doubts by assuring her that expressive art did not involve drawing anything recognizable. All she needed to do was make a few simple marks or shapes on paper. I gave her paper and pastels, and after a moment of focusing her attention on the place in her body where she was feeling that sense of confusion, Rachel drew three rows of continuous black and green loops (fig. 13). The body can't lie or reinterpret a feeling the way the mind can. Consequently, its experience of a feeling as expressed through a drawing is a more accurate representation than words of how we really feel about an emotionally charged situation.

I asked Rachel how it felt to draw her confusion. She smiled and said, "It felt strangely liberating. As soon as I began, I knew the drawing had to be done in those two colors—black and putrid green—because my confusion is two-sided, but for the first time I know what those two sides are. The black is my reaction to the dark side of my husband's deceptive behaviors. He lies about everything—the money he spends, where he goes after work. The green is the side representing the love I still feel for him. But it's a putrid green, because my love is sick and decaying."

Rachel stopped, looked at me wide-eyed and said, "I really do have to walk away and end this marriage. I can't stay in a decaying relationship. I have to sign those divorce papers. And what's more, I have to tell him, the way this drawing told me, that it really is over. Otherwise, I'll keep both of us going around in endless circles, just like the circles in this drawing."

When she finished talking, I asked Rachel how she felt. She said, "For the first time I feel relieved. Now I know why people say a picture is worth a thousand words."

Drawing what you feel is easy, quick, and immediately beneficial, because it allows you to release the hold those feelings have on your body and mind. In addition, your drawings will clarify what your feelings have been trying to communicate to you all along.

Imagery—the Inner Language of the Body-Mind

The expression, "One picture is worth a thousand words," was first coined by Fred R. Barnard in *Printer's Ink* magazine in 1927. When he wrote it, Mr. Barnard was afraid people wouldn't take it seriously, so he falsely attributed its origin to a Chinese proverb to give it more validity. What Mr. Barnard didn't know was that fifty-four years later, split-brain research would prove him right. A picture is composed of imagery, and imagery—a function of the right side of the brain—is the body-mind's internal, subconscious language; our primary form of

Figure 14: *Getting to the Heart of the Matter,* by Susan Fox

words. Its creator, Kina King, was having trouble explaining to our Drawing from the Heart group what her anger felt like. She started and stopped, then said, "It feels kind of like, well you know, all wishy-washy." We didn't know what she meant, but when she drew what that anger felt like, there was no doubt in our minds. Kina King's drawing certainly demonstrates the truth of Mr. Barnard's aphorism: a simple image can convey in a flash what would take a page full of words to describe.

communication. Words—a left-brain function—are a secondary form of communication. Every thought or feeling we have begins as an image. Unlike the left, verbal side of the brain, the right, imagistic side of the brain does not analyze or judge our experiences. It merely perceives and records them. This accounts for the major difference between what our words and images tell us.

The body is the experiencer of our feelings; the mind or left brain is the interpreter of our feelings. When we express an emotion as an image, we get an accurate representation of what we are really feeling. When we express an emotion in words, we get the left brain's judgmental interpretation.

An image can be a picture representing real objects as in figure 14, or it can be just a combination of abstract forms, shapes, and colors expressing a mood, feeling, physical sensation, or emotion. The image in figure 15 is an example of how abstract shapes, lines, and colors can represent a feeling far better than

What You'll Learn in This Program

In this program you are going to learn how to use your body-mind's inner language of imagery to express and heal your painful emotions through drawing. You will also learn how your inner imagery can help you identify what you are *really* feeling about any issue or problem in your life, rather than

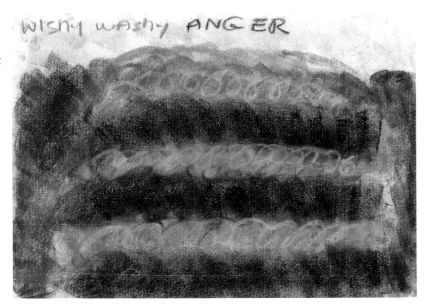

Figure 15: *Wishy-Washy Anger,* by Kina King

depending on what you *think* you feel. The processing questions following each drawing exercise will help you understand not only what you're feeling, but what to do about those feelings.

Drawing What You Feel Relieves Stress

Most people think stress is something that happens when they are overbooked, overworked, or overwrought with feelings that seem out of control. What really causes stress is a conflict between our thoughts and feelings. That conflict occurs when the body sends a clear *feeling signal* imploring us to say NO to something, while at the same time our thoughts send *verbal guilt messages* pushing us to say YES. Saying yes when we want to say no triggers what's called the stress response. That makes us feel agitated, anxious, cranky, and downright miserable.

Drawing reveals your inner conflicts. It also relieves your stress. When you draw an image of what you're feeling, the act of drawing releases that stress-producing feeling from your body, deactivating the stress response.

Drawing What You Feel Can Keep You Healthy

If you are dealing with emotional pain, whether it is extreme and disrupting your entire life or simply causing you to feel distracted and out of sorts, it must be released. Any painful emotional experience, especially one that is in conflict with your thoughts, will trigger the stress response. When the stress response is activated, stress hormones—adrenaline, epinephrine, and cortisol, among others—are released into the body, causing an increase in heart rate, blood pressure, perspiration, and muscle tension. These physiological stress reactions create the actual pain or discomfort we feel in the body when one of life's many events turns sour or even tragic.

If we don't release the emotions causing the pain, they will continue to activate the stress response, which depletes the immune system. Over time, unreleased stress-producing emotions produce chronic conditions like hypertension, heart palpitations, migraine headaches, neck and back pain, stomachaches, ulcers, and gastrointestinal disruptions, as well as general feelings of fatigue and malaise. Untreated, these conditions can lead to depression and eventually the onset of illness and disease.

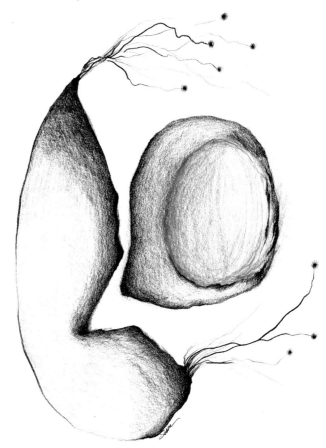

Figure 16: *Separation*, by Sabra Park

"This drawing expresses the anxiety I feel about my daughter moving back in with me. I don't really want to share my small space, and that makes me feel selfish. The image of separation represents the mother part of me, the nurturer of a child, from the nurturer of myself. The painful part that's pulled away has light. The part left is calm, reaching out at the ends."

7.19.00 Wow-really do need this art... all arts bring me into the Space -- that place where I'm just me. My core me, my center ... truly my Self. Via this drawing art, ■ that "quiet thing (the flow) happens + I actually look into [RIGHT here, a m'Work Title + idea struck - it's written in yellow paper: "A Trip thru me ... perspectives ... Et A."...] ! I feel a phyt and tumultuous emotion bubbling:

Figure 17: *Wow—Really Do Need This Art,* by Susan-Marie Beauchemin

How to Begin

This chapter will tell you everything you need to know to begin drawing from the heart. First I'll explain how the program works and why it's important to pace yourself as you go through the exercises. Then I'll give you some tips on how to get the most out of your drawing and healing experience. For those unfamiliar with art materials, I'll tell what you need to buy and how to select a place that's conducive to doing your healing work.

Think of This As an Exercise Program for Your Emotional Health

To get the most from this program, it might help to think of it as an exercise regimen for your emotional health. With that in mind you'll understand why it's important to follow the program exactly as it's set up. You wouldn't jump into an exercise program and start doing advanced reps without building up to them, nor would you expect noticeable results if you were not consistent with your exercise routine. Likewise, if you want to reap the emotional benefits, this healing program requires commitment and consistency.

How Much Time Do You Need?

Three days a week, half an hour a day, is ideal. Once a week for forty-five minutes or an hour per session would also work, but not as well. More time between sessions makes it difficult to get back to what you were feeling in the previous session. I wouldn't advise working on the exercises every day. That could short-circuit the results, leaving you feeling tired, overwhelmed, and emotionally drained. Allow a day or two between sessions to give your body and mind time to assimilate and integrate the emotions that surface.

How the Program Is Set Up

The program is divided into seven steps designed to take you gently and progressively deeper into the layers of your emotional pain. Therefore, it is vital to follow the program in order.

How to Achieve Positive Results

1. *Set up a schedule.*

   In any exercise program, it is consistency that yields success. To ensure consistency, designate a specific day or days of the week to practice the exercises. Set a start and finish time for each session.

2. *Write your schedule on your calendar.*

   If you don't write your schedule down, it won't happen. Having it on a calendar is also a reminder to those in your household that you are unavailable at specific times.

3. *Find a time to work when you won't be interrupted.*

   Turn down phones and answering machines; they can distract your concentration.

4. *Do the pre-exercise reading first.*

   Each step includes a brief introduction to the healing intention you'll be working on and an explanation of the goals of that step. It's important to take a few extra minutes to read through this material before you begin the exercises.

Figure 18: *The Wild Part of Me,* by Kate Siekierski

"She has fire burning inside—she's the wild part of me. She's alive. She's powerful. She's full of passion and desire. She's standing in water for balance. She wants more water. She has been wounded in the neck and chest. She seeks the water. As she reaches the river, she feels the cleansing of the water."

5. *Work with a therapist.*

Expressive drawing can bring up a lot of feelings and memories you may not be prepared to handle by yourself. Although you will learn how to lessen the emotional intensity of a painful memory or feeling if one does surface, you may need additional support. If you have painful unresolved issues or if you are dealing with a traumatic event, I recommend that you either work with a therapist or have one available as needed. If you are presently seeing a therapist, let her or him know that you are using this program. You may even want to bring your drawings to your sessions and discuss them.

6. *Be gentle with yourself.*

Healing takes time. Do not try to rush it. If you do the exercises in the first step and then find you need to take a break for a few weeks, do it.

BE DARING, LET LOOSE

My colleague Susan Fox is an expressive-arts educator and the coauthor of our book *Visual Journaling*. We do many of our workshops together, and the participants love it when Susan brings in her large basket of found objects—baubles, beads, trinkets, strips of colored papers and foils, wire, lace, gauze, glue, and scissors. Susan encourages them to push their emotional expression as far as their imaginations will take them. She then invites them to look into the basket and pull out anything that will reflect the imagistic messages that want to come through in their drawings, just as she does with her own work, shown in figure 19.

Susan did this drawing on a large piece of paper, then cut and reshaped it into twin snakes forming a semiheart shape. She glued a small decorative appliqué to the head of the snake on the left. To enhance the color of the snake's tail on the right, she added a red firebush leaf along with some dabs of glitter paint. She also glued a small eucalyptus leaf beneath the tail, which she says helps to anchor the form while still creating a sense of movement.

Remember, a drawing doesn't have to be limited to pastels or markers on paper. You can cut it, bend it, add to it, and shape it in any way that suits your fancy. Be daring, let loose, have fun—express yourself!

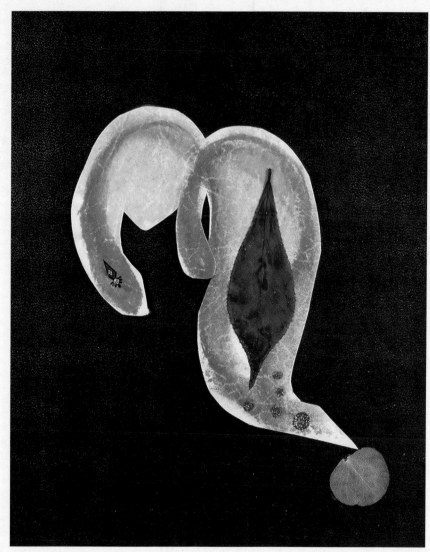

Figure 19: *Inner Creator*, by Susan Fox

What You Need to Begin Drawing from Your Heart

ART SUPPLIES

Here's a list of supplies that you'll need to start. Some items are essential, some optional, depending on preference and budget.

Essential Supplies:

- A sketch pad or hard-bound, lineless drawing journal, at least 8" x 10"
- A box of pastel chalks (the more colors, the better), or a box of crayons
- Scissors or an X-acto knife
- Masking tape
- A roll of paper towels

Optional Supplies:

- Colored markers
- Colored pencils
- A box of oil or water-based pastels
- Water-based glue
- A box of watercolors and brushes
- Bottles of colored glitter or tubes of glitter paint
- A variety of brushes

Most of these materials can be purchased at any art-supply store, most office-supply stores, and sometimes even drugstores.

ADD A LITTLE SPICE TO YOUR DRAWINGS

If you want to add a little spice to your drawings, brush on some glue—like Elmer's—to various parts and sprinkle a bit of sand or glitter while the glue is still wet. You can even use actual spices, like cinnamon, nutmeg, parsley, or chives to create some extra color and even stimulate your olfactory sense. You can also collect natural objects, like small shells, feathers, leaves, string, seeds, and twigs, to attach to your drawings. You can find ideal collage materials just lying around the house, like scraps of fabric, lace, yarn, cotton balls, gauze, or even aluminum foil.

A PLACE TO DO YOUR DRAWINGS

If you plan to use a hard-bound drawing journal or sketch pad that fits easily into your lap, you won't need more than a comfortable chair and good lighting to do your drawing exercises. If you use a large sketch pad or drawing paper, a sturdy table or drawing board is a must. The most important thing is to pick a space that's quiet, where you can be alone. It also helps if you can leave your art materials spread out so that you don't have to lug them around and set them up each time.

Figure 20: *My Heart Cracks Open to Release the Pain,* by Barbara Ganim

"The pain I held inside my heart for so long made it ache.
When I finally drew an image of those painful feelings being expelled from my heart,
the release was incredible. The pain just melted away."

Figure 21: *My Self Emerging,* by Joya Peterson

"This is a healing symbol. It shows my heart radiating the energy of every color with white at its core, because that reaffirms my oneness with God. I was not consciously thinking at the time I created this drawing about which colors to use. I knew that all the colors needed to be there in order for me to feel complete and whole, because all the bands of color in the heart are part of me. They emanate out from my core as an organic unfolding."

The Importance of Color in a Drawing

Nothing expresses an emotion or feeling quite like color. Color in a drawing can convey the subtlest physical sensations or the slightest energy shifts and impulses generated by an emotional response. Color is energy vibrating at a specific frequency. Energy is a part of all living beings. We are made up of an energetic system—an electromagnetic energy field—that runs through our entire physical body and extends outward beyond the body into what is commonly called our energetic aura. This energetic aura can be seen as pure color by those who know how to sense or observe it. Many people are also able to sense or envision the energy within their own bodies, such as the energy Joya Peterson, a member of my first Drawing from the Heart group, felt and expressed in her drawing in figure 21.

Some people are even able to tune into the energy fields of other people as well as the spirit energy of those who have passed on. The drawing in figure 22 shows how Susan-Marie Beauchemin used color to express the spirit energy of a departed loved one. As a way of dealing with the death and loss of her cousin Maurice, Susan-Marie invited his spirit to "visit." In a meditative state of open receptiveness, she connected to what she believed was his spirit energy. She then used color to draw the vibratory images that depicted what she had asked her cousin to show her— "where one goes after leaving the body."

Figure 22: *Maurice,* by Susan-Marie Beauchemin

" *I feel that the depth of subconsciousness reached while in the expressive-art process can contact the consciousness of those who have passed on. Two days after my adored cousin died, I asked him to enlighten me as to where one goes after leaving the body. Perhaps he came, perhaps this was done simply to heal my hurt. I believe it was a bit of both. Since doing this drawing, I have felt peaceful regarding his death. Though it is a loss, I have not felt emptiness or gnawing from his departure. I have not had a need to shed tears. And I know he remains available should I need his wisdom.*"

Color Transcends Verbal Thoughts

Color is a powerful communication tool that transcends our verbal thoughts in a way that is both immediate and responsive to our deepest feelings. Color is a universal communicator. The drawing shown in figure 23, by Sandra Salzillo-Shields, a former graduate student and now a professional artist, is an example of how someone can be moved to express a feeling through color and form, and yet have no idea what that feeling is until the image begins to appear on the paper. Although the message inherent in the image itself seemed clear to Sandy as soon as she drew it, it took months before she understood that the color green represented her heart chakra—the place within the body where we hold unconditional love, which can help us to heal ourselves and others.

How Color Facilitates Transition through the Healing Process

Color is a highly individualistic form of expression. There is no formula for its use and no preordained method for interpreting its meaning. Appreciating the role color plays in the healing process cannot be fully achieved by looking at one isolated drawing an individual produces while working through the many layers of emotional pain. Therefore, when each of my Drawing from the Heart support groups ended, I asked the participants to bring in all the work they had done. This enabled them to see not only the progress they had made drawing and healing their pain, but also how the drawings evolved and connected to each other. That's when it became clear to them that color was the most vital factor in facilitating their healing process. With this in mind,

the remainder of this chapter displays a series of drawings by three individuals whose work illustrates how color influenced their healing process while working through the seven steps of this program.

Figure 23: *In My Ending Is My Beginning*, by Sandra Salzillo-Shields

"This image came to me intuitively while my sister was undergoing a mastectomy for breast cancer. I had no preconceived idea of what I would draw. It's almost as if this visual intention floated into the room and I grasped onto it for a second, and within that second all the elements of the image and the colors were there. It wasn't until several months later that I realized that green was the color of the heart chakra—the seat of unconditional love and healing. I realize now that this piece of artwork was the physical manifestation of my prayer for my sister's healing."

Jan

During her first few weeks in the support group, Jan's drawings were rendered in dark, dismal colors to express the anger and pain she had been feeling for years. Just when it seemed that her palette would never change, she came into group with several new drawings composed of luminous hues that appeared to dance on the paper. She told the group that if she had continued doing those dark drawings, even though she still had more anger to express, she would have gotten stuck there. She needed to move beyond it, so she allowed herself to connect instead with a feeling of healing energy that she knew existed deep inside her. Two of those drawings, shown in figures 24 and 25, demonstrate how color helped her express that healing energy.

Another piece Jan did in this series was a drawing/collage (fig. 26) that became the ultimate symbol of healing for her. The intention was to create a drawing/poster that imagistically transformed her fear-based, negative beliefs into positive, empowering beliefs. To do that, Jan incorporated a color

Figure 24: *The World through Rose-colored Glasses,* by Jan

"Because my previous drawings were so dark and intense, I decided to use every bright color in my box of oil crayons as I doodled. Although I had no particular intention as I began drawing, the feeling I get now looking at this drawing is that these are all the colors in nature—the life force. And that's what life is, and that's what I would like my life to be. It's what the world would look like if I allowed myself to see it through rose-colored glasses."

29

Figure 25: *Healing Energy,* by Jan

"This drawing began with a circle, and then I just continued to let it flow and expand. It started off as a drawing of grain. I see grain as very nurturing. I love the way grain blows in the wind. It forms a vortex in the center. This is an image that represents my energetic expression of physical and emotional healing. I would like to put this on my bedroom ceiling so that I could look at it every night and remember how good it feels to feel good."

photograph of herself with photo clippings of roses cut into the shape of butterfly wings glued onto a background in which she drew a multicolored rainbow, a waterfall, raindrops, a golden path, and mountain tops upon which she can dance and soar.

Jan attached the image of herself with wings to a paper tab that allowed the figure to move up and down and side to side—so that it could dance on the poster's surface. Jan said this poster was her symbol of power, because it represented all that she loved about herself—that part that comes alive most when she is dancing.

Figure 26: *Feeling Free at Last,* by Jan

"The images in this poster are metaphorical. The waterfall represents cleansing. The raindrops react with the sun to create the rainbow. There is a golden path for me to follow no matter how steep the mountains. The upper wings of the butterfly are flowers in full bloom. I have a golden halo representing a state of grace. The rainbow represents the gift we receive when we can balance the light and dark sides of ourselves. The sun is the passion that fuels us. I am standing on solid ground with trees and grass all around, a symbol of life. There are gold nuggets scattered about, because the riches of the earth lay at my feet. The movable body represents my freedom to go wherever I choose. I have a see-through skirt on, because I no longer have to be ashamed of my body. This poster reminds me that I am capable of soaring."

Figure 27: *Soul Spiral,* by Birgitta Grimm

"My soul feels walled in; it cannot expand. The red is my fear—invasion. The yellow is power—light. The blue is peace. The pink is lightness. The transparent places are joy, expansion, and hope."

Birgitta Grimm

Birgitta Grimm is an artist who had worked in a variety of art media for years. However, using art to heal her emotional turmoil was a new experience that began when she was diagnosed with breast cancer in 1993. That's how I first came to know Birgitta—she was a member in one of my Healing with Art cancer support groups. Birgitta and I stayed in touch with one another through the years. Just as I was about to begin my first Drawing from the Heart support

Figure 29: *A Magical Place*, by Birgitta Grimm

"I saw a bright and gleaming triangle surrounded by light, water, trees, and life—a magical place—a place I did not want to leave."

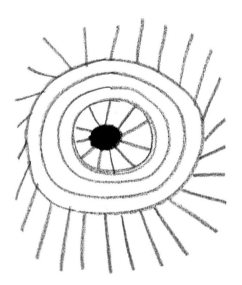

Figure 28: *Terror*, by Birgitta Grimm

"When I focus on my illness, I feel the pain of terror. It is a downward spiral that will not allow me a way out. When I think of terror, I think of falling into a well—dark with no light; being alone without air. My breath is taken away. This drawing took me to breathlessness. My heart center felt panic. I wish I could find a way out of the dark circle."

group, Birgitta was diagnosed with a recurrence of cancer that had metastasized into her bones and lungs. She wanted to join the group, but was unable to attend the Tuesday evening sessions. She asked if I would e-mail the drawing exercises to her so that she could follow the program on her own. I was happy do it.

As she completed the exercises, Birgitta sent me color copies of her drawings and her written responses to the processing questions. As I looked at them, I was struck by her use of color. Drawing was Birgitta's salvation; color was her primary means of expression. Her progress as she worked through the exercises was so remarkable that I wanted to include several of them here.

Birgitta began the first exercise of the program by identifying what she needed to heal: "I want to work on my fear that this recurrence is going to take me to a place of pain and terror. I am afraid of the cancer taking over my body and of losing my grip on my life. I also want to work on the anger that sometimes swells up inside of me, but sadness is the most overwhelming feeling."

Figure 30: *Being Supported,* by Birgitta Grimm

In the next exercise, Birgitta drew an image that represented what her soul was feeling in the midst of this cancer recurrence. (See fig. 27, *Soul Spiral*). It exemplified how the soul can feel our pain, but unlike the mind that becomes overwhelmed by that pain, the soul can also feel the power to survive and find peace within the storm.

After identifying terror as the predominant emotion associated with her illness, Birgitta drew an image of what her terror felt like in her body. This drawing (fig. 28) had only two colors, black and purple, which exemplified how restrictive and imposing this feeling was.

To transform her terror, Birgitta did another drawing (fig. 29). This drawing served as an inspirational image to keep in her heart as a symbol of hope, healing, and empowerment. The colors vibrate with light and energy. Notice how she used many of the same colors as those used in *Soul Spiral.*

The next drawing Birgitta did surprised her. The image (fig. 30) started out, so she thought, to be a star, but it progressed into a flower. She then intended to draw stars around the flower, and they too turned into flowers connected through gossamer strands supporting the center flower—a powerful metaphor representing the support she knew was always around her. This drawing reminded her that she could rely on the abundant support that was hers for the asking from family and friends, as long as she remained connected to her feelings. If she disconnected from her feelings, as she had been doing up to this point, no one could help her, because they wouldn't know she needed their support.

Nicki

Like Birgitta Grimm, Nicki was also struggling with pain and fear brought on by her second experience with cancer. Seven years after her first bout of breast cancer, Nicki was diagnosed with a new cancer in the other breast. Also like Birgitta, Nicki had been a member of my earlier Art and Healing groups. When I learned about Nicki's recent diagnosis, I invited her to join my Drawing from the Heart support group.

At first, Nicki found it difficult to connect with her body's experience of an emotion. Although she knew intellectually that she needed to heal her feelings of anger and loss, Nicki had trouble getting in touch with how her body reacted to those feelings. Nicki was patient with herself. As a result, she was finally able to move her awareness below her shoulders into her gut where her anger had lodged. That's when an image of her anger finally came through in a multicolored drawing that astonished not only the group, but Nicki as well (fig. 31).

Figure 31: *Anger,* by Nicki

"Pain, loss, and hate are at the root of my anger. It's always been hard for me to express anger, because it feels so out of control. This drawing felt like such a release to finally just let it out. As I drew, I went from being out of control to feeling more in control."

35

anger fuels the power

ready to take flight

anger transformed = power, strength, direction, freedom

an arrow that becomes a wing

May 30, 2002

Figure 32: *An Arrow that Becomes a Wing,* by Nicki

*"Anger fuels the power of an arrow ready to take flight. Anger transformed equals
power, strength, direction, and freedom."*

When Nicki began working on figure 31, there was a powerful energy behind the movement of her hand as it
scribbled overlapping circles on the paper. It was an energy that I had never observed in her drawing technique.
Usually her drawings were gently executed with a kind of slowly modulated self-control. But now there was no
self-control. It was as if all her previous restraints were broken and the raw energy of her emotions poured out
onto the paper. As she talked about that drawing, what amazed her most was that it was only after *being willing* to
surrender control that she was able to get it back. "Now," she said, "my anger feels empowering." As a follow-up,
Nicki did a transformational drawing (fig. 32 above) that expressed her feelings of empowerment.

Figure 10: *The Heart Speaks,* by Diana Boehnert
(For a discussion of this picture, see page 13.)

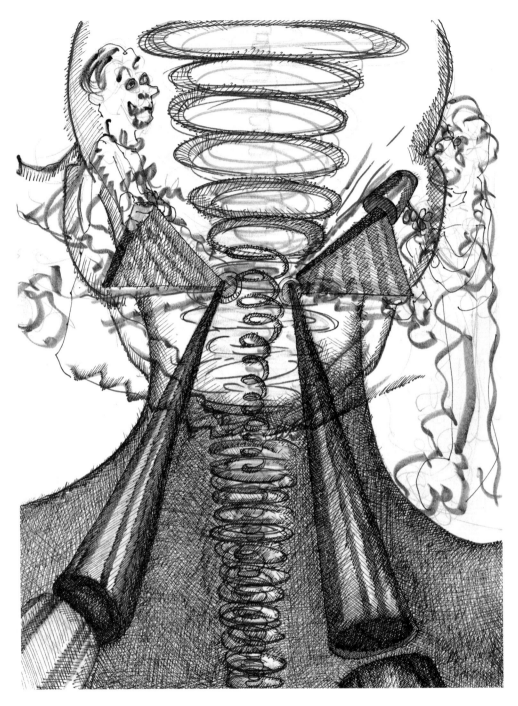

Figure 33: *The Pressure to Conform to the Will of Others,* by Barbara Ganim

*"The silent urgings of others to be what they expected of me, was causing excruciating pressure
at the base of my neck. It felt like people were driving wedges into my head—pounding and pushing relentlessly.
Just drawing that feeling was enough to relieve the pain."*

An Introduction to the Seven Healing Steps

Figure 34: *I Need to Heal My Fear of Love,* drawing by former client

The exercises for the seven steps in this program begin in Part Two. They will guide you through the healing process of drawing from your heart. In Step One, you will decide what needs to be healed. Step Two will help you identify the most predominant emotion associated with the painful issue or experience you plan to work with in the program. Then you will be introduced to the three basic stages of healing with art. In Step Three, you will learn how to deal with your feelings of loss.

Step Four will help you get to the root of the fear your loss has produced. Step Five will show you how to uncover the emotions that lie beneath your guilt. Step Six will introduce you to the power of forgiveness and its role in the healing process. In Step Seven, you will draw healing images from your heart. With each step, you will explore a different aspect of the painful issue or experience you are working with as you move deeper into the layers of your pain.

Figure 35: *Breaking Out,* by Lisa Maciejowski Gambuzza

"This is a representation of the shuttered windows I grew up behind during childhood. Beyond the shutter, life blooms, out of reach, held back, beckoning to be lived. I mentally threw a chair through this screen to open my shuttered self."

Figure 36: *Helpless,* by Kris Hall

"I see the lines fanning out from each side of his little face as angel wings protecting him. The glowing arch encircling the top of his head is telling me that God is with him and me, regardless of what happens. This drawing tells me that we are both being taken care of."

Processing Questions

Every drawing exercise will be followed by a set of processing questions designed to help you understand the meaning of your drawings. It's best to write your responses to these questions as soon as you complete an exercise while you're still feeling the effects of the drawing experience. Writing your responses rather than just thinking about them enables you to go back later and see what you were feeling when you worked on each exercise. It also makes it easier to track your healing progress.

Deciding What to Heal

The key to deciding what you need to heal in Step One is to trust whatever issue or experience presents itself, even if you already have something else in mind. Frequently, people come into my groups intending to heal the painful emotions provoked by a major issue in their lives. Yet they quickly find themselves focusing on something less significant. At first, they think they are merely allowing themselves to be side-tracked by minor issues that they are inclined to dismiss as "no big deal." I always advise them to go where their hearts have led them. Invariably, they soon realize that the smaller issue is not only linked to their major issue, it provides the one piece of information or the perspective they need to deal with the larger issue.

When Kris Hall first came into the support group, she wanted to work on a painful issue from her past, but her little Shih Tzu dog, Ruggie, was sick, and she was afraid he would die. She asked if it would be all right to focus on healing her feelings of helplessness around Ruggie's illness instead of the bigger issue. I encouraged her to trust her need to begin working with her feelings about her dog's illness.

After identifying her predominant emotion as helplessness, which she wrote on the top of her drawing paper, Kris drew an image representing how her soul was feeling about this situation (fig. 36). She told the group that just drawing that image made the fear and helplessness subside. In the coming weeks

Figure 37: *Love & Spirit Shih Tzu God,* by Kris Hall

Ruggie's condition worsened, and Kris had to have him put down. Returning to group, she told us that losing her dog brought her full circle to the issue she originally intended to work on when she joined the group. With both circumstances in mind, she did another drawing to transform her feelings of helplessness. That drawing (fig. 37) helped her heal the feelings from both experiences.

When Your Pain Feels Overwhelming

If your emotional state is so fragile that deciding where to begin feels too overwhelming, it may be easier to start out by not thinking about the specific circumstances that created your pain. Concentrate instead on the feeling sensation of the pain inside your body and the words that would best describe that pain, such as *anger, rage, sorrow, hopelessness,* or *depression.* As you work with the feelings and begin to express and transform them, the details of your experience will become less important and less overwhelming.

Important Points to Remember As You Begin Drawing from Your Heart

THERE IS NO WRONG WAY TO DO IT.

There is no wrong way to draw from your heart. Stick figures, wavy lines, drawings that look like they were done by a five-year-old work just as well, if not better, than a beautifully rendered drawing. When you get too caught up in how a drawing *should* look, the pureness of the emotional expression can be lost.

YOU ARE THE ONLY ONE WHO KNOWS WHAT YOUR DRAWINGS MEAN.

Only *you* know what your drawings really mean. Never allow someone else, even a therapist, to interpret your work. With this program, you will learn how to do that for yourself using the processing questions that follow each drawing exercise.

WHAT IF YOU HAVE NO IDEA WHAT YOUR DRAWING MEANS?

As you begin trusting your initial responses to the processing questions, you will be surprised at just how much you really do know about your drawings.

NEVER TRY TO INTERPRET SOMEONE ELSE'S DRAWING.

If you are doing this program with a friend, avoid the temptation to throw in your two cents about what *you think* someone else's drawing might mean, even if your opinion is asked.

STAY OUT OF YOUR MIND.

As you respond to the processing questions, stay out of your mind. That is, don't think about your responses, feel them. If you find yourself saying, *I think this drawing is telling me . . .* , stop and rephrase that into a feeling statement, like this: *I feel that my drawing is telling me . . .*

TRUST YOUR INTUITION.

Always trust the first thought that comes to you when you respond to the processing questions.

IF YOU SENSE RESISTANCE IN YOURSELF TO EXPLORE A CERTAIN ISSUE OR EMOTION— THEN DON'T!

If you feel uncomfortable exploring a certain issue or emotion, trust that feeling. It may mean that your body-mind is not ready to process it. When the time is right, you'll know because you'll feel it.

A Few Suggestions about the Exercises

Since every exercise consists of both written and drawing responses, you may want to work with two side-by-side pages. That way, one side can be your writing page and the other your drawing page. Figure 38 is an example of how a former graduate student, Susan-Marie Beauchemin, used a double-page spread while working on an exercise from the book *Visual Journaling*. Notice how Susan-Marie indicates the date at the top of her writing page and what the exercise is about, along with the exercise page number. You may want to do that as well, so that you can look back later and know exactly what you were working on. Sometimes Susan-Marie preferred to integrate her words and images on one page, as in Figure 39.

Working on Large Sheets of Drawing Paper

Some people are uncomfortable with sketch pads or drawing journals, and prefer instead large sheets of drawing paper. If you are so inclined, use the top of your drawing paper to write the date, the intention of the exercise, and any verbal responses the exercise calls for. You can keep a separate notebook to answer the processing questions, or, if you prefer, write your responses directly on the drawing.

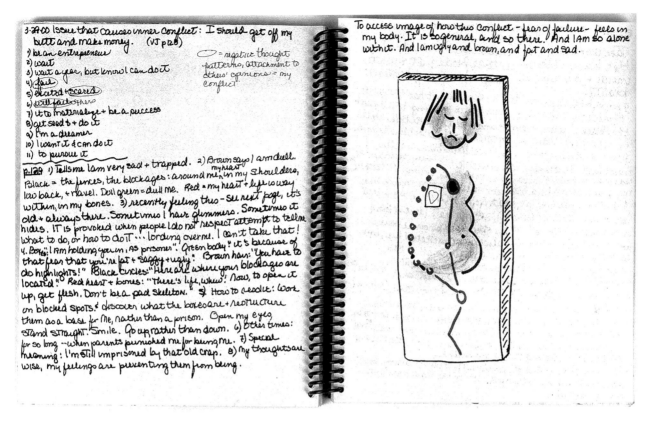

Figure 38: *Issues that Cause Inner Conflict,* by Susan-Marie Beauchemin

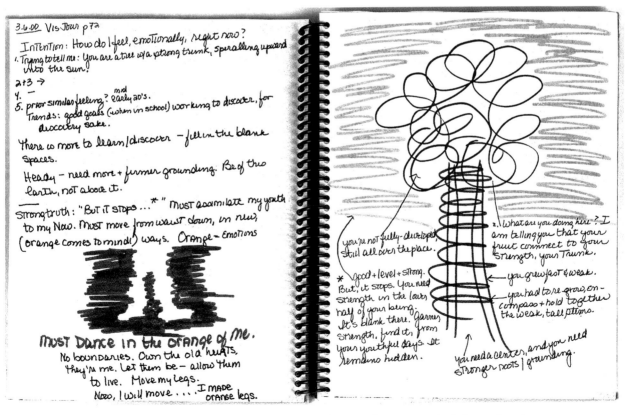

Figure 39: *How Do I Feel Emotionally, Right Now?* by Susan-Marie Beauchemin

THERE ARE NO ACCIDENTS IN EXPRESSIVE DRAWING

I believe that everything in a piece of artwork has meaning, whether we understand it or not. A squiggle usually appears in a drawing for a reason, as does a smudge or a tear. The placement or position of an object or an image can also be important. A haphazard series of squiggles on the bottom of your drawing could represent the unruly parts of your life you may be trying to push down or out of the way. A series of flowers could symbolize certain people in your life. The same could apply to a random grouping of stars, clouds, bushes, trees, or even mountains in the distance. Let no smudge go unexplored.

An example of a meaningful accident can be seen in a drawing by group member Craig MacDonald. When Craig began working on this drawing (fig. 40), he wanted to express the anger he felt in his heart.

Figure 40: *My Heart Begins to Open*, by Craig MacDonald

"I was drawing my anger when the paper tore and it felt like a crack opened in my heart. As I kept drawing and tearing more paper, more anger got released. Looking at this drawing now, I know what the tearing was all about. My heart was beginning to open."

He began using watercolors to lay down large shapes. As he felt the anger coming through his fingers, he switched to pastels so that he could press harder. He felt this helped push the anger out of his body onto the paper. Soon, the paper began to tear. At first, Craig thought he had ruined his drawing. He wanted to throw it out and start over. I reminded him that there are no accidents and asked if that tear might mean something. He wasn't sure yet. He wanted to keep working into the tear.

I handed him more paper to place beneath the torn drawing, and encouraged him to keep going. He continued to press and push the pastels through the tear, making marks on the sheet of paper beneath it until that sheet ripped too. He kept drawing, letting the energy of his anger spill onto the next sheet of paper. Finally he stopped and said it was done. I asked if he knew now what those tears meant. He nodded and said, "When the paper tore, it felt like a crack opened in my heart and the anger just poured out. Tearing the paper made that possible."

Figure 41: *Layers of Pain*, by Jan

"When one is angry, layers of the body and mind begin to fuse together, just like in this drawing. The layers build upon each other like emotional contagion. I didn't know I was still feeling all of this. I finally had to stop doing this kind of drawing because I couldn't be in that emotional space anymore."

Another group member, Jan, did a drawing that also started to rip and peel beneath her oil crayons. Working on a large pad of newsprint, as her drawing (fig. 41) began to tear, she continued drawing onto the page below. When it tore, she still kept drawing. After drawing and tearing through several layers of paper, she applied poster paint, allowing it to seep through each layer, cementing them together. Although the layered affect of the completed drawing was not intentional, Jan felt that the cemented layers represented how energy within the body and mind fuses together when anger is not expressed and released.

Figure 42: *I Am Alive*, by Kate Siekierski

PART TWO

Exercises
for the Seven Steps

Figure 43: *I'm Here to Heal My Heart*, by L.T.

Identifying What You Need to Heal

Emotional healing cannot begin until you have clearly identified what you need to heal. In this first step you will start by writing down exactly what you want to heal in your drawing journal or sketch pad. This is called *setting your healing intentions*. It gives concrete form to your conscious thoughts. An intention, once set, will serve as an inner directive for your body, mind, and spirit, guiding all three elements to activate the healing process. The second exercise will help you compare what your thoughts, as evinced through the words you wrote, tell you about the pain you wish to heal, and how your soul (or heart) feels about your pain as revealed through the image in your drawing. This will enable you to spot any conflicts that might exist between what you *think* about your pain and how you *feel* about it. Since inner conflict is the main source of physical and emotional stress, it's important to at least recognize it.

As you read the directions for the exercises, you will see an occasional **TIP**. This will be a pointer to help clarify a particular aspect of the instructions or a reminder to guide you where you may have doubts about how to proceed or questions about the directions.

EXERCISE ONE

Setting Your Healing Intentions

When you are ready to begin this first exercise, place your drawing materials in front of you. Get into a comfortable position in a chair or on the floor. You may want to put on some soft music and even light a few candles or burn a little incense—whatever helps you set a contemplative mood. Then read the following directions as they guide you through this first exercise. As the exercises continue, I will abbreviate the directions.

- Close your eyes and clear your mind of all thoughts about what you think you *want* to heal, and ask yourself instead what you *need* to heal.
- When you know what that is, open your eyes and write it at the top of your drawing paper or on the drawing page of your journal or sketch pad. Leave enough room beneath it for the second exercise.

> **TIP** *Keep in mind that you can't heal an experience, such as a divorce or an argument. You can only heal yourself and the emotions or feelings that the experience produced. So be sure that what you write reflects your need to heal some aspect of yourself and/or certain feelings and emotions.*

Expressing Your Feelings through Images

Emotional pain affects not only your physical body and the way you think, it affects your soul as well. In the first exercise, I asked you to verbally identify what you need to heal. In this next exercise, you will learn how to express your feelings through images—the inner language of your body, mind, and spirit. As a starting point for exploring the depth of your emotional pain or discomfort, I'll guide you through the process of connecting with your soul's voice—a voice that speaks through images, not words—to see how your soul feels about what needs to be healed. This drawing will become a marker or baseline of how your soul feels now as you embark on the healing process. At the end of this program, you will be instructed to do another drawing of how your soul feels, so that you can compare the difference between the two.

Figure 44: *The Tender Sunshine, the True Self,* by Jan

"I desire to be free of the angry, hopeless, helpless feelings that gnaw away at my insides. The image in the drawing is me feeling fragmented and jumbled. I labeled it The Tender Sunshine, The True Self, *because deep in my heart a light glows no matter what chaos is going on around me."*

ACCESSING AN IMAGE OF AN EMOTION USING BODY-CENTERED AWARENESS AND VISUALIZATION

To do the drawing exercises in this book, you'll be using two techniques: *body-centered awareness* and *visualization*. These techniques will help you disconnect from your mind's interpretation of the pain you wish to heal and connect instead to the way your body experiences that pain.

Body-centered awareness shifts your attention away from your thoughts to your physical body. The easiest way to do that is to focus on your breathing.

Visualization means to picture or imagine what the feeling sensation caused by an emotion would look like if you were to express it as an image. I prefer to use the word *imagine*, because many people get intimidated by the term *visualize*. They are afraid they won't be able to see an image when they try to do it. Some people actually do see an image in their mind's eye when they focus on the feeling sensation produced by an emotion. Other people only sense what a feeling would look like; they don't actually see anything when they close their eyes. There are also people who get in touch with what an emotion feels like, but have no idea what it looks like until they begin to draw. There's no right or wrong way to imagine what an emotion looks like. As you start to do this process for yourself, you will discover what works best for you. Trust your instincts.

EXERCISE TWO

Drawing an Image of How Your Soul Feels about the Pain You Wish to Heal

This is your first expressive drawing exercise. Do this drawing on the same page or paper you used to write your healing intention. The goal is to imagine an image that represents how your soul (or heart, if you prefer) feels about the pain you wish to heal. The directions below will lead you through the exercise.

- Close your eyes, take three deep breaths and slowly sigh them out. Then breathe normally for a minute or two, and as you do, focus your attention on your breath. As you continue to breathe, become aware of the rest of your body.
- With your eyes still closed, focus your awareness on the place in your body where you sense your soul might reside, or focus on your heart center. As you focus on this place in your body, ask your soul or heart to present you with an image that represents how *it* feels about your pain. When you know what that image is, open your eyes and draw it.
- If an image does not come to you, just open your eyes and begin to draw what you imagine your soul or heart is feeling.
- When you have completed the drawing, spend a few moments looking at it along with what you wrote about your healing intentions from the first exercise.

Processing Questions

The following questions will help you recognize any conflicts between how your soul or heart feels about what you wish to heal, and how your mind interprets what you want to heal.

As you read through these processing questions, take the time to respond to them in writing. Writing your responses will help you go deeper into your feelings than just thinking about the answers.

TIP *Always trust your first impressions when you respond to the processing questions.*

1. What did the healing intention you wrote in the first exercise tell you about your mind's interpretation of what it *thinks needs to be healed?*

2. How did it feel to do the drawing of how your soul or heart responds to your pain?

3. Do you see any conflicts between what your words tell you about what needs to be healed, and what your soul or heart tells you through your drawing?

4. What do your colors reveal about what your soul or heart feels?

5. Are any details, squiggles, or smudges in your drawing trying to tell you something?

6. If your drawing could speak, what would it say about the way your soul or heart reacts to your pain?

7. What have you learned from your drawing about the pain you wish to heal?

8. Why has it been difficult for you to talk about the issue or experience causing your pain?

THE DIFFERENCE BETWEEN OUR WORDS AND IMAGES CAN REVEAL INNER CONFLICTS

T he drawings in figures 45 and 46 were done by two members of my support group. They are good examples of the kinds of conflicts that can occur between our thoughts and feelings, which are readily revealed when we compare the differences between our words and images.

Neither Debbie Northup nor Nicki was surprised by the pain, negativity, and fear their words revealed when they wrote what they wanted to heal. However, they were astonished by the positive, hopeful messages conveyed through the images in their soul drawings. Once we understand the nature of the conflict between our thoughts and feelings, it is much easier to reconcile them.

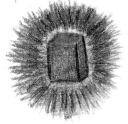

I would like to get rid of the terrible ache that I feel. The hurt and pain of years of lies and pretending.

4/23/02

Figure 45: *Healing Intentions & Soul Drawing,* **by Debbie Northup**

"Although my words said I want to get rid of the terrible ache I feel, I drew an image of my soul as a small patch of blue inside a garbage can. I drew it that way because I feel like I've been tossed into the garbage by certain members of my family who cannot see me for who I really am. In this drawing, my soul turned into a brilliant blue light shining inside the can and all around it. To me, that means that my soul knows the truth. It continues to shine its light, even though some people will never see or appreciate it."

Figure 46: *Healing Intentions & Soul Drawing,* **by Nicki**

"My words told me I needed to heal the fear and sadness I was feeling going through my second bout with breast cancer, but my soul gave me a different message through its image of this purple waterfall. Drawing the image felt good, like there was a power inside me after all. I knew that my soul was telling me that I would be okay, and that the fear and sadness will pass through me just like this waterfall."

Accessing, Releasing, and Transforming the Primary Emotion Causing Your Pain

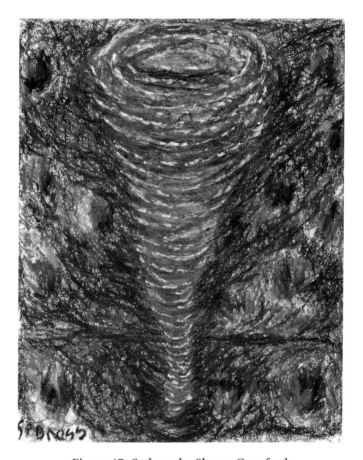

Figure 47: *Sadness,* by Shawn Crawford

"Although anger is the primary emotion I feel the most, deep down in my heart, I know that what I really need to heal is my sadness, my disappointment, and that feeling of chaos. It feels like a whirling tornado deep inside my soul."

It is important to identify the primary emotion you associate with the issue or experience causing your pain; otherwise your focus gets scattered. Even though you may be feeling many different emotions, there is usually one BIG ONE that is most disturbing. The first exercise in Step Two will help you identify that one big emotion. Once you know what that is, the two exercises that follow will take you through the three basic stages of healing with art to access, release, and transform that emotion.

If You Have Difficulty Identifying a Specific Emotion

Mary Ellen Madsen, whose drawing can be seen in figure 48, was a Drawing from the Heart support-group member. When I presented this first exercise in Step Two to the group, Mary Ellen had difficulty identifying one specific emotion connected to the divorce she was going through. She told the group that when she tried to do this exercise, *pain* was the only word she could think of.

As you begin this exercise, you may feel the same way. If so, don't worry about trying to come up with a specific emotion. Although pain isn't an emotion, it is always prompted by at least one emotion, even though you may not know what it is. The emotion associated with your pain will likely emerge as you begin to draw.

Figure 48: *Pain,* by Mary Ellen Madsen

EXERCISE ONE

Identifying the Most Painful Emotion Associated with What You Wish to Heal

- Close your eyes and think about the experience or issue causing pain in your life. Allow the emotions connected to this situation to surface. As they do, allow yourself to become aware of the most significant or painful emotion you associate with this situation. When you know what it is, open your eyes and write one word (if possible) that identifies it.
- Beneath your word(s), write one sentence that explains how this emotion affects you and your life right now.
- Write one sentence explaining why it hurts to talk about it.

WHAT YOUR WRITTEN WORDS CAN TELL YOU

The way in which you write the word(s) identifying an emotion can tell you a lot about how your mind reacts to a painful experience—which can be quite different from how your body reacts. When you have written the word(s) identifying the primary emotion associated with your pain, take a moment and look at the way you wrote those words on your paper. Then think about the following questions:

• Were the letters you used to write your word(s) big or small?

• Where did you place your word(s) on the page or paper?

• Did you scrawl your word(s) across the entire page in big, bold letters, or did you use tiny letters squeezed into one corner or a small segment of your paper or drawing journal?

• Did you use a pen or pastel chalk, a crayon or a marker?

• If it was chalk, crayon, or marker, what color did you use?

• Did you use more than one color?

What do your answers to these questions mean? You may find that sometimes they mean nothing at all. But more often than not, where you place your word(s) on the paper may indeed be related to where you place this emotion in your life. Big, bold letters dominating the page may mean you are allowing this emotion to dominate your life. Tiny letters squeezed into a corner may mean that you are pushing this feeling off to the side. Only you can know if there is any meaning behind the way you wrote the word(s) identifying your painful emotion. If you sense there might be some significance to the way you wrote your word(s), jot down your thoughts, using the previous questions as a guide. Your responses may offer insights into the way your mind reacts to this emotion.

Reread the two sentences you wrote beneath your word(s) explaining how this emotion affects you and why it hurts to talk about it. What does the way you wrote this tell you? For example, does anything strike you as interesting about the size or placement of your words in relation to the word(s) you wrote identifying your primary emotion? How about the color(s) you used to write them? Jot down any thoughts you might have about these questions.

EXERCISE TWO

Accessing and Releasing an Image of Your Painful Emotion

If you have verbally identified the primary emotion associated with what you wish to heal, you are ready to begin accessing and releasing it. Accessing the way an emotion feels inside your body is the first of the three basic stages of healing with expressive art. Releasing it is the second stage. That takes place when you draw an image that represents what that emotion feels like in your body. The third stage is transformation. You will be guided through that process in Exercise Three.

<u>TIP</u> *To help you remember the three stages of healing with expressive art, I developed an acronym: ART*

*A*ccess an image of a stress-producing or painful emotion.

*R*elease that image through expressive art.

*T*ransform a painful image into a new image that represents a less stressful, more positive way to respond to whatever causes your pain.

• If you are ready to begin, get comfortable. Allow yourself to disconnect from your thoughts by focusing on your breathing. This will bring your awareness into your body.

• Focus your attention on the painful emotion you identified in the previous exercise. Allow yourself to tune in to how this emotion feels inside your body. Notice the place or places where you experience the feeling sensation of this emotion. Let your awareness move into that part of your body. Become aware of how this emotion feels.

• Imagine what this feeling would look like if it were an image. What colors best express how it feels? What shapes or forms best express it?

• When you know or sense what this emotion would look like as an image, open your eyes and draw it.

• If an image does not come to you, then just open your eyes and draw what that emotion feels like, using whatever colors seem to best express that feeling sensation.

• When you have completed this drawing, spend a few moments looking at it along with what you wrote about this emotion in the first exercise. Then respond in writing to the processing questions.

Processing Questions

1. *Is there a difference between what your words told you in Exercise One about how your thoughts respond to this emotion and what your body tells you about its response through your drawing?*

2. *What did it feel like to do this drawing?*

3. *How does your body feel now?*

4. *What does this drawing tell you about how your body reacts to the experience producing this painful emotion?*

5. *What do the colors you used tell you about your reaction?*

6. *Are any details, squiggles, or smudges in your drawing trying to tell you something about your reaction?*

7. *If this drawing could speak, what would it say to you?*

8. *Would you like to change the way you react to this painful emotion into a response that feels less stressful? If so, why?*

Healing Begins with Transformation

The act of accessing and releasing a painful emotion through drawing may make you feel better by moving that stress-producing image onto the paper, but it does not mean that you have healed or resolved it. Resolution of an emotion or the experience producing it isn't always possible. (Sometimes there simply is no way to resolve a painful experience, such as loss of a loved one or a traumatic occurrence like an assault, accident, or a life-changing illness. However, you can heal the pain by transforming or changing the way you react to it.) Transformation, the third stage of healing with art, involves asking your heart for a symbol that represents a more positive and peaceful way of reacting to a painful, stress-producing emotion.

Changing Your Reaction to a Painful Emotion Does Not Mean Ignoring It

Although you cannot change the event that caused your painful emotion, you can always change how you react to it. Just remember, changing your way of reacting does not mean ignoring your painful emotion. What it does mean is choosing to experience it differently—in a way that is less emotionally charged or even toxic to your system. What's important to understand is that you can be sad without becoming immobilized, and you can be angry without feeling like you are about to explode. The choice of how you experience any emotion is always up to you.

Figure 49: *Transformation of the Pain,* by Mary Ellen Madsen

"This is the transformation of the shattered landscape of my marriage. Everything softens and blends together, the shattering sun turns into a heart. This feels good, even though the pain is still there. That's okay, because I know it has to be. The heart in this drawing tells me that I can make it through; I am strong and capable, and most importantly, I can heal."

To Change Your Response to a Painful Emotion, Change Your Image Association

Change doesn't happen by simply telling yourself that you want to change—you must also change the image your body-mind associates with that painful emotion. The image you drew in Exercise Two is the image you presently associate with your painful emotion. This image triggers your body's stress response. To deactivate that trigger, you have to change the image that represents the way you respond to the emotion causing your pain. The next exercise will take you through the process of changing or transforming that image.

EXERCISE THREE

Transforming Your Response to Your Painful Emotion

- Close your eyes, take a few deep breaths, and focus your attention on your body by concentrating on your breath. When you feel connected to your body, allow your awareness to move into your heart center.
- Ask your heart for a symbol that represents a gentler and more constructive way of reacting to the painful emotion you identified in Exercise Two.
- When you know what this transformational symbol is, draw it.

> TIP *If a transformational symbol doesn't come to you, open your eyes and take whatever color pen, chalk, or crayon seems to convey the feeling of calm and peacefulness that you would like to experience. Use it to draw that feeling. If you can keep your thoughts and judgment out of the way and trust the drawing process, a symbol will emerge. Let your feelings guide you as you draw.*

Processing Questions

1. *How does it feel to look at this drawing?*

2. *How did it feel to do the drawing?*

3. *How is this transformational symbol drawing different from your first drawing?*

4. *What is this symbol trying to tell you about how to transform the way you respond to your painful emotion?*

5. *If this symbol could speak, what would it say to you about the situation that sparked your painful emotion?*

6. *What do the colors in your drawing symbolize?*

7. *Do any of the shapes, forms, or details convey a special meaning or message about this new way of responding to your painful emotion?*

8. *How might this new way of responding change your actions and behaviors when dealing with the situation or issue that provoked your pain?*

EXERCISE FOUR

Understanding What Your Painful Emotion is Trying to Teach You

Emotions are messengers. Their persistent proddings can give us essential information about ourselves. They warn us when we are in danger. They alert us when we ignore our personal feelings and needs. They help us make the right choices and decisions as we go through our lives. Emotions are truly our most valuable teachers. Their lessons can transform us at a core level by opening our hearts to love and forgiveness. They can reveal our greatest strengths and our deepest fears, and at the same time show us how to overcome those fears. This exercise will help you get to the core of your lesson by encouraging you to look to your heart for a symbol that represents it.

> TIP *Assuming that you now know how to connect with your body, I will skip the lengthy instructions in the exercises and go directly to the point in the remaining exercises of the book. If you forget how to access an image of an emotion or feeling, you can always refer to Exercise Two in Step Two (page 55).*

- Connect with your body and focus for a moment or two on the feeling sensation produced by the painful emotion you've been working with.
- Then shift your awareness into your heart center. Ask your heart to present you with a symbol that represents what this painful emotion has to teach you.
- When you know what that symbol is, draw it.

Processing Questions

1. How does it feel to look at the drawing of your heart symbol?

2. What does this symbol tell you about the lesson of your painful emotion?

3. How do the colors in your symbol relate to this lesson?

4. Do any of the details, squiggles, or smudges in your drawing suggest something important about this lesson?

5. How can you apply this lesson to your life as well as the experience producing your painful emotion?

Drawing through a Stroke

Most people draw *after* a painful experience has occurred, but not artist Riva Leviten, who kept on drawing—not one, but three separate drawings—while she was in the middle of two cerebral strokes (figures 50, 51, 52). Riva has been a friend for over thirty years, and during that time I've come to admire her determination to stick with things no matter what—but drawing right through a stroke raises the bar of stick-to-itiveness to a whole new level.

At seventy-four, Riva is still drawing and making prints, even after the strokes, which required over a month's stay in a rehab facility. When she called to tell me about the three drawings, which she believed helped her to survive those strokes, I asked her permission to feature them in this book. She was delighted and hoped that they would help people to know that neither age nor strokes can limit one's ability to create art that informs and heals the self.

Figure 50: *Omen,* by Riva Leviten

Figure 51: *Deity Uno,* by Riva Leviten

Figure 52: *Zenith*, by Riva Leviten

"I was working on all three drawing collages when I had two small strokes in April 2002. Although my head was pounding, I kept drawing, motivated by a force I wasn't familiar with. I was compelled, biting my lip to control my confusion. There was something about the circular nature of these images that could be, in a sense, mundane, but the collage element added to the image called 'Omen' looked to me like a chopped word that spelled out Na or No. The belly-buttonlike shape in the middle of 'Zenith' seemed like a howling face opening up to the universe. Was this the face of an omnipotent God, or me questioning the pain, I wondered. After the arrival of these poignant portraits, I called 911."

Ask heart to present me w/ a symbol of the life lessons this loss is trying to teach me

Draw the symbol Dialogue w/ drawing What is color, shape telly me.

What do you want me to know? How can I put this lesson into application

bloom   open up to the light   beginning   freedom

Figure 53: *What My Loss Has Taught Me,* by Nicki

"Just when I think I've lost my ability to trust my body because of the cancer, this drawing reminds me that my body didn't betray me. This second experience with cancer opened me up like this blooming flower, so that I could see the light—get the message, once and for all. The lesson I'm meant to learn is that I have an opportunity and the freedom to try for a new beginning."

Acknowledging and Transforming Your Loss

To heal any kind of loss, you must first acknowledge that you've suffered one. While that may seem simple enough, there are times when people are completely unaware that they have even experienced a loss. If you don't know what you've lost, you can't transform it, and you certainly can't heal the pain it creates.

Every painful experience produces loss of some sort. Every life-changing event—even the good ones, like a joyfully anticipated marriage, the birth of a child, the opportunity to travel, a new job, or a promotion—can also produce losses as we move on and leave people and places of importance behind. Tangible losses, like the loss of a loved one, a job, a home, a community, or a valued possession are easy to recognize and acknowledge. They had form and substance. They were here, and now they are obviously gone. Intangible losses are more difficult to recognize, because they consist of ways of thinking and feeling that exist only in our minds and hearts. Intangible losses include loss of faith in God, loss of trust in ourselves or others, loss of hope, courage, ambition, creativity, spirit, independence, and security, to name just a few. When such losses occur, they can eat away at our souls.

Intangible losses are the hardest to heal, because they can hide for years beneath denial, anger, and avoidance. Without realizing it, an intangible loss can color our thoughts and influence our actions. It can keep us from pursuing new relationships, jobs, and opportunities that can enrich our lives. It can cloud judgment and change a previously happy, light-hearted person into a bitter and cynical ogre.

Step Three will help you recognize and acknowledge any tangible or intangible losses that were created by your painful experience through completion of a sentence stem. Sentence stems are a form of verbal brainstorming that can help you dig deep into your subconscious to identify losses of which you may not be consciously aware. Once you've identified what you've lost, you will pick one loss to work with in the remaining exercises. In the second exercise, you will access and release an image that represents how this loss feels when you think about it. The third exercise will help you transform your feelings by asking your heart for an image that represents its perspective on your loss. In the fourth exercise, you will continue the transformation process by asking your heart for a symbol that represents the lesson of your loss.

EXERCISE ONE

Identifying and Acknowledging Your Losses

• With your eyes closed, think about the painful situation or experience you have selected to work with. As you do, write the sentence stem below on the top of your journal, sketch pad, or drawing paper.
• Complete the sentence stem with any loss-related endings that pop into your mind.

When I think about my situation, it hurts to know that I've lost . . .

• If you think of only one loss, that's fine.
• If you have more than one loss, pick one to work with in the remaining exercises. Write it on another piece of drawing paper or a new page in your journal or sketch pad.

> <u>TIP</u> *Write down any loss that comes to mind, even if it seems insignificant or unrelated. If you thought of it, trust that it is important. Don't edit yourself or judge your choices.*

EXERCISE TWO

Drawing an Image of How Your Loss Feels

What you think influences how your body feels and the way it responds to a painful situation. This exercise will help you draw an image of the pain your negative thoughts create in your body.
• Close your eyes and focus on the loss you wrote down in the previous exercise. Think about that loss and how it makes you feel. As you begin to sense those feelings, notice where in your body those feelings are coming from. Move your attention into that place (or places).
• Concentrate on that feeling sensation, then imagine what that feeling would look like if it were an image. When you know, draw it.

Figure 54: *Feeling Orphaned,* by Debbie Northup

"I have lost trust in my family of origin. I feel orphaned. In this drawing, I am facing a path that I will have to walk alone. It's a scary path, and there is no one to show me the way. I began navigating this path when I was a little girl, and as a woman I am still walking it alone."

Processing Questions

1. *Where in your body did you feel your loss?*

2. *How does your body feel now that you did this drawing?*

3. *What does this drawing tell you about how your body reacts to your thoughts about your loss?*

4. *What do the colors tell you about your reaction?*

5. *Are there any details, squiggles, or smudges that might be trying to tell you something about the way you react to your loss?*

6. *If this drawing could speak, what would it say about the way you experience your loss?*

EXERCISE THREE

Transformation: Drawing Your Loss from Your Heart's Perspective

In this exercise you will ask your heart for an image that represents its perspective on your loss.
  • Close your eyes and connect with your body. Shift your awareness into your heart center. Ask your heart to present you with an image of how it perceives your loss. When you know what this image might be, draw it.
  • When you finish your drawing, compare it to the drawing you did in the previous exercise. Then answer the questions that follow.

Processing Questions

1. *How does this drawing make you feel as you look at it?*

2. *What's the difference between the drawing of your heart's perspective on your loss and the drawing in the previous exercise?*

3. *If this drawing could speak, what would it tell you about your heart's view of your loss?*

4. *What do the colors tell you about the way your heart responds to your loss?*

5. *Are there any details in your drawing that might be trying to tell you something more about your heart's response?*

6. *What did you learn from this drawing?*

EXERCISE FOUR

What Your Loss Is Meant to Teach You

• Connect with your body and focus on your feeling of loss. Shift your awareness into your heart center. Ask your heart to present you with a symbol of what your loss is trying to teach you. When you know what this symbol might be, open your eyes and draw it.

Processing Questions

1. How does this drawing of your heart's symbol make you feel?

2. What do you feel this symbol tells you about the life lesson of your loss?

3. How do the colors relate to your life lesson?

4. Are any details in this drawing trying to tell you something?

5. How can you apply the lesson of your loss to your current life as well as to the experience that produced it?

Seeing the Gain, Not the Loss

The goal of the exercises in Step Three was to help you see, through the eyes of your heart, what you've gained instead of what you've lost. Although your loss may have left a scar deep on your heart, the heart can reach beyond the scar to embrace and hold dear whatever the loss has given you. This is called *the gift of the experience.* Shifting your perspective from loss to gain can strengthen and fortify you for the rest of your life. Staying focused on the gain instead of the loss is the only way to keep yourself open and receptive to new people and experiences, even though you know you cannot hold onto them forever.

Getting to the Root of Your Fear

Figure 55: *The Fear of Opening My Heart,* by L.T.

"When I think about opening my heart, I am afraid that I'll be hurt; God will hate me; I'll be alone; I'll die. At the root of my fear is the negative belief that, if I am true to myself, I'll be hurt. If I show them who I am, I'll be hurt. God doesn't love me, want me. Life is dangerous; I have no protection."

Fear comes from many sources, but the fear that comes from emotional pain runs deep into the heart and soul of each of us. It hits hard and stays put, shaking the foundation of all we have come to know and trust in ourselves and others. Where there is pain, fear is sure to follow. If we don't get to the root of its cause and change it, it will follow us all the days of our lives.

Some fears are instinctive, while others are learned. As children we learn not only to fear others, but also to fear our own inadequacies. It's the rare child who hasn't heard a myriad of negative messages that he or she will carry for a lifetime. *You'll never amount to anything. Who do you think you are? You can't do that, so don't even think about it.* Such messages form a deeply ingrained root system of self-limiting beliefs that can produce an overgrown, out-of-control thicket of fears. When pain and loss occur in our lives, fear kicks in, making our recovery far more difficult.

For each of us, the negative beliefs and thoughts that create the roots of our fears are different, so we must dig deep to expose them. Once exposed, those roots can be transformed into new beliefs that are more positive, loving, and hopeful. As a child, you had little choice but to accept the beliefs passed on to you. As an empowered adult, you can construct your own beliefs. Positive beliefs create possibilities. Negative beliefs create impossibilities. If the negative

roots of your fears are replaced with positive messages, your fears will be transformed into life-altering assets.

Step Four will help you identify the fears your pain and loss have germinated in your own nutrient-depleted soil of negativity. Once you have identified them, you will draw an image representing what those fears feel like, as if they were weeds growing in the garden of your life with their roots extending deep into the contaminated, lifeless soil that spawned them. You will then be asked to write about the negative beliefs that have encouraged the growth of your fears in the space around their roots. Next, you will transform those life-defeating fears into life-enhancing assets by rewriting your negative beliefs as positive beliefs. As a final step, you will then create a poster/drawing made up of images or symbols that express and reinforce your new positive beliefs.

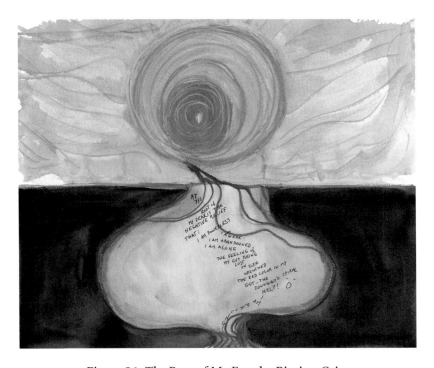

Figure 56: *The Root of My Fear,* by Birgitta Grimm

"When I think about my cancer, I am afraid that I will lose control, that I will have pain, and that I will be helpless—a burden. I am also afraid that I will be weak and I will fall. In this drawing, my symbol of fear is a red-hot circle radiating throughout my body up to my heart and down to my feet. At the root of my fear is the belief that I am powerless, weak, abandoned, alone, and falling."

EXERCISE ONE

Identifying the Fears Your Pain and Loss Have Produced

• The following sentence stem will prompt your thoughts about the fears your pain and loss have produced. Write it down and complete it with any fear-based endings related to your pain. If you can think of only one fear, that's fine.

When I think about my loss, I am afraid that . . .

EXERCISE TWO

Drawing the Roots of Your Fears

• Begin by drawing a light pencil or chalk line across the center of your paper to indicate the space above and below the ground. Focus on either one or all of the fears you identified in the first exercise. Connect with your body to access an image of what your fear feels like. Use the space above the ground line to draw that image of your fear as if it were an out-of-control weed in the garden of your life. Use the space below the ground line to draw the roots of your fear. Leave some empty space around your roots to write the negative beliefs that have created your fear.

• In the space around your fear roots, write the following sentence stem:

At the root of my fear is the belief that . . .

• Complete it with as many negative-belief endings as possible.

Processing Questions

1. *Were you surprised by the fear(s) your painful situation has provoked? If so, why?*

2. *Has this fear come up before? If so, when?*

3. *Where in your body did you feel your fear?*

4. *Do you have any physical ailments in that part of your body?*

Figure 57: *Getting to the Root of My Fear: Powerless,* by Nicki

"My fear feels like a fog in the dark. I can't see what's ahead. At the root of my fear is the belief that I'm powerless to have the future I want."

TIP *What the mind represses, the body expresses. Physical ailments often develop in the part of the body where unexpressed feelings are left to fester. Accessing and releasing those feelings through drawing can help alleviate those ailments.*

5. *What did it feel like to do this drawing of your fear?*

6. *What does this drawing tell you about how your fear has affected your life?*

7. *What do the colors tell you about your fear?*

8. *Are any details in your drawing trying to tell you something about your fear?*

9. *If this drawing could speak, what would it say?*

10. *Did the negative beliefs you identified as contributing to your fear surprise you? If so, in what way. If not, why?*

Transforming Your Fear through Cognitive and Imagistic Restructuring

If you would you like to change the way your fears are affecting you, you need to change the beliefs that created them. As you now know, that kind of change needs to include both cognitive and imagistic restructuring. Cognitive restructuring means to change your negative beliefs into positive beliefs. Imagistic restructuring means to change your negatively charged, fear-producing image associations into positive, self-empowering images.

Figure 58: *Transforming My Fear: Wild Hair,* by Nicki

"This drawing says that I can have the future I want. This heart symbol is what will enable me to let go of my need to be perfect, because that's what blocks my ability to have the power and the future I want. I need to stretch, use my energy to open up and move. This drawing feels powerful, reaching with my body, expanding the possibilities. I have wild hair in this drawing, because who doesn't want wild hair? It's not perfect. I think of the expression 'Letting your hair down.' You can't be perfect when you let your hair down."

EXERCISE THREE

Creating an Empowerment Poster

• To restructure the negative beliefs that created your fear(s), look at the negative beliefs you identified in the previous exercise. Rewrite them as positive beliefs. Use large colored markers or pastels or oil crayons to rewrite your negative beliefs as positive, empowering beliefs in big, bold letters anywhere on your poster.

> <u>TIP</u> *For this exercise, I recommend using large drawing paper or poster board (at least 18 X 24 inches) so that you can integrate your written beliefs with your positive images as a poster. Making a poster that you can put on a wall where you'll see it every day will help replace your negative beliefs with your new, empowering positive beliefs and images.*

• Spend a few moments looking at the positive beliefs you wrote on your poster. Then close your eyes and ask your heart to present you with an image or symbol that best expresses the power and positivity of each new belief. Draw those symbols on your paper or poster, integrating the image with the words you wrote.
• Feel free to incorporate other media, such as paint and/or collage materials.
• When you have completed your poster, put it up and look at it for a few days before responding to the processing questions that follow.

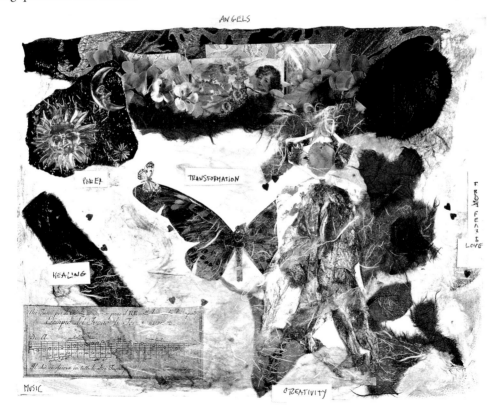

Figure 59: *Transforming the Roots of My Fears,* a drawing/collage poster by Birgitta Grimm

"I am strong, courageous, able, full of hope, powerful; I am full of love. Transformation: from fear to love; from feeling stuck to being creative; being surrounded by angels; being protected."

71

Processing Questions

1. *How did it feel to change your negative beliefs into positive beliefs?*

2. *How did it feel to draw the images or symbols that your heart envisioned for each new positive belief?*

3. *How do you feel when you look at this poster?*

4. *How would it affect your fears if you were to incorporate the messages in this poster into your life?*

5. *Was there anything that surprised you as you rewrote your negative beliefs as positive beliefs?*

6. *Was there anything about the heart images or symbols that surprised you?*

7. *Do any details in your poster suggest symbolic meanings or messages?*

8. *What did you learn from this exercise?*

Figure 60: *Transforming My Fear*, by Jeannine Gendron

"This imagery started out as just a black spot, which is what fear felt like inside of me. It transformed as I gave it my attention, not by giving it power, but by using my power to overcome and change it. It was a very transforming event to make this imagery."

Guilt: Uncovering What Lies Beneath

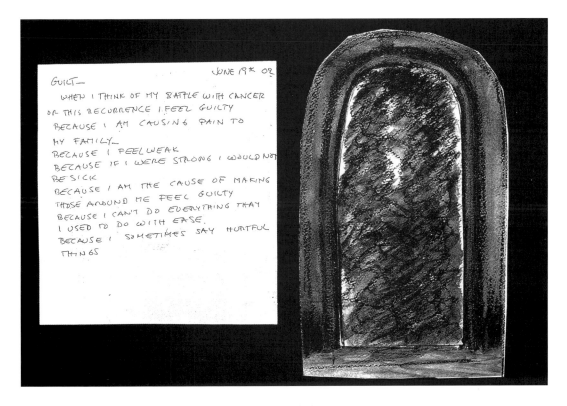

GUILT—
JUNE 19th 02
WHEN I THINK OF MY BATTLE WITH CANCER
OR THIS RECURRENCE I FEEL GUILTY
BECAUSE I AM CAUSING PAIN TO
MY FAMILY.
BECAUSE I FEEL WEAK
BECAUSE IF I WERE STRONG I WOULD NOT
BE SICK
BECAUSE I AM THE CAUSE OF MAKING
THOSE AROUND ME FEEL GUILTY
BECAUSE I CAN'T DO EVERYTHING THAT
I USED TO DO WITH EASE.
BECAUSE I SOMETIMES SAY HURTFUL
THINGS

Figure 61: *The Vine of Guilt,* by Birgitta Grimm

*"My guilt is like a vine growing over a doorway. It keeps me from opening the door
to see what's really under there."*

Guilt is a cover emotion that we use unconsciously to cover up or conceal emotions we are not in touch with or that we are not yet ready to recognize, accept, or divulge. As long as we stay focused on how guilty we feel about something, we never have to deal with other feelings—the feelings that lie hidden beneath the guilt.

Guilt stands in the way of the healing process, because it keeps us from getting to those deeper feelings—feelings that must be acknowledged and dealt with before we can move on. The key to working with our guilt is to uncover the emotions that lie beneath it. Once uncovered, we can decide on a conscious level whether or not to act on those emotions or transform them into another way of reacting that is more acceptable.

It's important to remember as you uncover the emotions lying beneath your guilt that you needn't act on them. Sometimes that isn't possible. Recognizing the emotions beneath your guilt and integrating them into your thought process is what's essential when it comes to healing the pain they have created.

There are few painful experiences in which guilt is not a steady companion. When we're embroiled in a painful experience it's difficult to acknowledge our real feelings. The exercises in Step Five will help you identify and express feelings of guilt provoked by your painful experience. They will also help you uncover the real emotions that lie beneath your guilt, so that you can choose to resolve or transform them.

EXERCISE ONE

Identifying Your Guilt

• To uncover the real emotions hiding beneath any guilt surrounding your painful issue or experience, you need to identify what you feel guilty about. To do that, complete the sentence stem below with as many ending as come to mind.

When I think about my painful experience, I feel guilty because . . .

• Go on to the next exercise.

Figure 62: *Web of Guilt*, by Nicki

"When I think about my cancer recurrence I feel guilty because I think could have done more; I didn't learn my lesson; I didn't take it seriously enough the first time. My guilt has created a flimsy spider web growing over the door that hides my real feelings. That web is mysterious and intricate."

Figure 63: *Honey of a Guilt,* by Debbie Northup

"My guilt is like sticky honey dripping all over the doors to my real feelings. It's like honey, because I have not been sweet enough to members of my family. That guilt sticks to everything in my life. My mother wanted me to be sweet and that undermined me emotionally."

EXERCISE TWO

Drawing Your Guilt As a Cover Over the Door to Your Real Feelings

- Lightly draw the outline of a doorway on your drawing paper.
- Focus on your feelings of guilt. Notice the feeling sensation that guilt produces in your body. Imagine what it would look like if it were covering the doorway to your real feelings. Draw that image of your guilt as well as the doorway it is covering.

Processing Questions

1. *How do you feel about the image you drew of your guilt as a cover-up?*

2. *Were you surprised by this image? If so, why?*

3. *Do you feel that the image of your guilt might have a symbolic or metaphoric meaning? If so, what would it be?*

4. *If the image of your guilt could speak, what would it say?*

5. *What did you learn about yourself by doing a drawing of your guilt as a cover-up for your real feelings?*

6. *What was the difference between what your words told you about your guilt in Exercise One and what your image tells you in this drawing?*

EXERCISE THREE

Drawing the Real Feelings Beneath Your Guilt

- Use an X-acto knife or scissors to cut open the doorway on your drawing paper. Tape another piece of paper beneath the open door.
- Ask your heart for a symbol that represents the feelings your guilt is covering up. When you know what that symbol is, draw it inside the opening of the doorway.

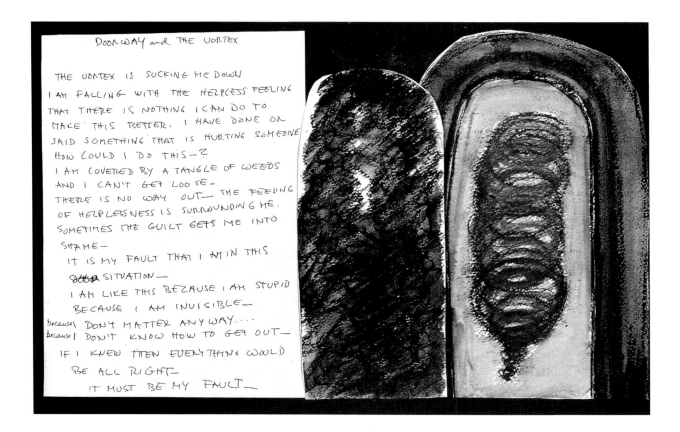

Figure 64: *Doorway and the Vortex,* by Birgitta Grimm

"When I imagined opening the door beneath the vine of my guilt, I saw a vortex. It was sucking me down, because I felt as if there was nothing I could do to make this better. This image told me that the real feeling beneath my guilt is that this cancer must be my fault."

Figure 65: *The Empty Bowl,* by Nicki

"The symbol I saw behind the door was an empty bowl. That bowl represents my feelings of scarcity, that feeling that I can't nourish myself and that there is nothing I can do, because I can't have what I want. But this drawing made me realize that it's not all up to me. I'm not responsible for everything."

Figure 66: *Beneath the Guilt,* by Debbie Northup

"Behind my doors, I saw an image of myself with a big X over it. That's because I'm not as sweet as my family wants me to be. That makes me feel nonexistent and unacceptable. But deep down, I know that I'm a good person, and I am acceptable to myself, and that's what's really important."

Processing Questions

1. *What hidden feelings does this symbol represent?*

2. *Were you surprised by this symbol?*

3. *Were you surprised by the feelings you have been hiding beneath your guilt? If so, why? If not, why?*

4. *If this symbol could speak, what would it say?*

5. *Are you comfortable with your real feelings? If so, why? If not, why?*

If you are comfortable with the feelings you've uncovered beneath your guilt, you're ready to move on to Step Six. If you feel uncomfortable with them, you may need a little guidance from your heart to find the best way to handle them. If those emotions are in conflict with certain aspects of your life that cannot be changed or that you don't want to change, your heart can also help you with that. The next exercise will give you a new perspective on the feelings you've uncovered beneath your guilt.

EXERCISE FOUR

Asking Your Heart for Guidance with the Feelings You Uncovered beneath Your Guilt

• On the top of your drawing paper, write down the uncomfortable feelings you uncovered beneath your guilt. Look at what you wrote down and notice how your body feels as you focus on it. Then bring your awareness into your heart center. Ask your heart for a symbol that represents what *it* wants you to do about the discomfort. When you know what that symbol is, draw it.

Processing Questions

1. *How does your heart symbol make you feel?*

2. *If this symbol could speak, what would it say about the feelings beneath your guilt?*

3. *Based on this symbol, what does your heart want you to do about these feelings?*

4. *How do the colors in your symbol relate to your heart's message?*

5. *Are there any details in your drawing that may be trying to tell you something important about the feelings your guilt was covering?*

6. *How can you apply your heart's message to the experience you have been working to heal in this program?*

7. *Can you remember other times in your life when you felt these same feelings? If you do, what was going on then? Was it related in any way to this experience?*

Connecting with Unhealed Emotions from the Past

The last processing question was intended to help you connect with any unhealed emotions from the past that may be linked to your present experience. The feelings guilt covers up are usually related to painful past experiences that produced emotions that were never dealt with at the time. As Step Five revealed, the guilt covering those feelings is often just too massive and entangled to allow you to see and release them. Discovering your unhealed feelings from the past and understanding their connection to your current experience can help you to see how these unrecognized feelings continue to incite painful reactions.

With only two more steps to go in the program, you are nearing the end of the healing process. If your response to that last processing question revealed a link between past and present feelings, it may be helpful to take a broader view of yourself as you complete the remaining exercises. However, it's not essential to the healing process to know the exact link between what you are working on now and the past. What is important is to be aware that emotional responses have cyclical patterns. If you make a conscious effort to recognize your emotional patterns, the healing you do now will reach deep into your subconscious to heal you at a core level.

Figure 67: *The Emotional Block to Forgiveness,* by Mary Ellen Madsen

"The block to forgiveness for me was fear—the fear of forgiving someone who could continue to hurt me. It was like a mountain I couldn't get past."

Forgiving Yourself and Others

I like to think of forgiveness as the peak experience of the healing process, because it is the pinnacle of the upward journey we must make in order to heal. However as singer-songwriter Paul Simon says, "the nearer your destination, the more you're slip-slidin' away." When it comes to forgiving, whether it's ourselves or others, nothing could be closer to the truth. The work you did in Steps One through Five is a piece of cake compared to how hard it can be to forgive those who have caused your pain.

Why is it so hard to forgive? After all, it's easy when you think about it: you can do it all by yourself, because the person you are forgiving never has to know. You can put it in a prayer, say it in a letter that you never mail or whisper it to the wind. It doesn't matter how— you just need to decide to do it, and then do it. Ah, there's the rub—doing it. Deciding and doing are not the same thing.

When the time comes to actually *do* the forgiving, to set the intention, to utter the words, most of us get trapped in that space between deciding and doing. What traps us? An emotional block! Even when we do the work necessary to heal the wounds created by a painful experience and we're finally ready to forgive, suddenly we find ourselves face-to-face with a mountain-sized emotion that we somehow missed in all that healing work. How did that happen? It happens because missing it is also part of the healing process. As we begin healing, we need to remove each layer of emotional pain before we can get to the core where that last bastion of emotion lives. We can't just dive straight in, hoping to hit it at first strike.

If you have completed all the exercises in the program, you are now near the core of your pain. But before your work is done, you have one more emotional excavation to complete. You need to dig down into your subconscious and unearth that one last emotional block that can prevent you from doing that final act of healing—forgiving those who have hurt you, including yourself.

EXERCISE ONE

Identifying Whom You Need to Forgive

- Think about someone connected to your painful issue whom you need to forgive. It could be more than one person or it could be yourself. Write down whomever it is on a piece of drawing paper or in your journal or sketch pad, and go on to Exercise Two.
- If there is no one you need to forgive, then do the optional exercise following Exercise Two to discover any emotional blocks that might stand in the way of your healing.

Figure 68: *My Emotional Block to Forgiveness,* by Birgitta Grimm

"There is an emotional block that keeps me from forgiving myself and others. It stops me from accomplishing the true healing of my spirit and soul. The block feels like a square with deep red drops of blood seeping or streaming and bubbling out and down to a puddle. The rectangle in the middle contains an orange creative spiral trying to escape."

EXERCISE TWO

Draw an Image of Your Emotional Block to Forgiveness

• Focus your attention on each person you want to forgive. Visualize that person. Notice the feelings beginning to surface as you think about forgiving that person. Focus your attention on those feelings—they are creating your emotional block. Draw what that block would look like if it were an image. If you have more than one person to forgive, you may want to draw a separate image for each person. If it's a group of people, like family members, you may need only one block.

Processing Questions

1. *Were you surprised at the person or persons you wanted to forgive? If so, why?*

2. *Were you surprised by the image of the emotion or feeling blocking your ability to forgive? If so, why?*

3. *How did it feel to draw this block?*

4. *What does this image tell you about your inability to forgive?*

5. *What do the colors you used tell you about your block?*

6. *Are there any details in your drawing that are trying to tell you something about your emotional block?*

7. *If this drawing could speak, what would it say?*

> TIP *Even if you did Exercise Two, you may want to do the upcoming Optional Exercise to see if you have any other emotional blocks that might prevent you from healing.*

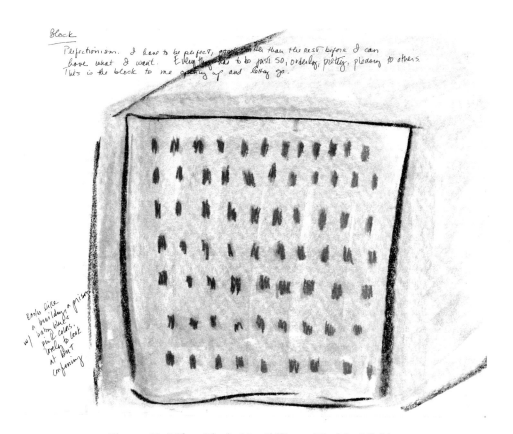

Figure 69: *What Blocks My Ability to Heal,* by Nicki

"Perfectionism. I have to be perfect, good, better than the rest, before I can have what I want. Everything has to be just so, orderly, pretty, pleasing to others. This is the block to my opening up and letting go. The image looks like a prison building. The colors are like a child's colors, baby blue and pink. It's lovely to look at, but confining."

Nicki couldn't think of anyone she needed to forgive. However, she did have a block preventing her from healing. That block was perfectionism. Nicki did the following optional exercise and drew an image of her emotional block (figure 69). This image helped her to see that as comforting as her perfectionism was at times it was also confining, and that confinement was keeping her from having the future that she wanted and healing the way she needed to heal.

OPTIONAL EXERCISE

Drawing Your Emotional Block to Healing

If there is something you know you need to do to heal, but you can't seem to do it, try this exercise. You may have an unrecognized emotion blocking you.

- Write down at the top of your paper or drawing page a few words that describe what you are having trouble doing, such as healing, changing, letting go, moving on.
- Close your eyes, focus on what you wrote, and notice how your body responds. If you feel discomfort or tension, that is the emotional source of your healing block. Imagine what that feeling would look like as an image, then draw it.

Processing Questions

1. *Were you surprised at what you identified as blocking your ability to heal?*

2. *Did your image surprise you? If so, why?*

3. *How did it feel to draw this image?*

4. *What is this image telling you about your block?*

5. *How does your body feel now that you did this drawing?*

6. *What do the colors in your drawing tell you about your reaction to this emotional block?*

7. *Are there any details in your drawing that might be trying to tell you something about your reaction to this emotional block?*

Figure 70: *Heart Symbol to Move Past the Block,* by Birgitta Grimm

"The symbol my heart gave me to move past the emotional block I have to forgiving myself and others is an orange spiral surrounded by a light pink, orange, and gold glow. It is expansive. Being able to sing with the joy of true love and light, that is the way to forgiveness. Here there are no restrictions of secrets and lies, no constrictions."

EXERCISE THREE

What to Do to Move Past Your Emotional Block

• Close your eyes and bring your awareness into your heart center. Focus your attention on the emotional block you just drew in either of the previous exercises. Ask your heart for a symbol that represents what you need to do to move past this block. When you know what it is, draw it.

   <u>TIP</u> *If you did both Exercise Two and the Optional Exercise, ask your heart for two symbols: one to move past the block to forgiveness and the other to move past your emotional block to healing.*

Processing Questions

1. How does it feel to look at your drawing of this symbol?

2. How did it feel to draw it?

3. If this symbol could speak, what would it say?

4. What do the colors in your drawing mean?

5. Are there any details in this drawing that might mean something to you?

6. How can you put your heart's advice into action?

   This concludes Step Six. The next and final step in this healing program involves creating healing images. This is the fun part of the program. The hard work is over, and it's time to put the icing on your healing cake.

Creating Healing Images from Your Heart

Figure 71: *Exuberantly,* by Kathleen L. Mack

"After my father died suddenly, I had so much grief and anger! As I drew this, my energy transformed, releasing that grief and anger, which allowed me to relish his life and his influence on me."

The word *heal* is derived from the same root as the words for "whole," "health," and "holy." Healing takes place when we accept and integrate into our psyches as well as our lives the fragmented and wounded parts of ourselves that became disowned, denied, or unacknowledged. Accepting all parts of ourselves without shame, guilt, or rebuke makes us whole. Restoring ourselves to wholeness is the key to optimal physical and emotional health. Wholeness in body and mind enables the spirit—the true essence of the self—to be fully expressed. When the spirit is released from the bondage of emotional pain and repression, the sacred part of the self—the soul—can emerge unfettered, free at last to enact its divine purpose in life. This is the holiness that emanates from the healing process—the reconciliation of our secular humanness with our divine sacredness.

Healing is often an indescribable phenomenon that involves a noticeable shift in the way we think about ourselves. It is the ultimate stage of transformation in which we begin to see ourselves differently. Healing, as you hopefully know by now, is more than just a state of mind. It affects the body and spirit at a deep and profound level that can be accomplished only by transforming your inner vision of yourself. To achieve this final phase of the healing process, you must replace the wounded images of yourself that were created by your emotional pain with new images that represent your enlightened state of mind, body, and spirit.

In this final step of the program, you will create healing images that represent your transformed vision of yourself as healed, whole, healthy, and holy. You will begin with an image of how your soul (or heart, if you prefer) feels now that you have completed the healing process. That image can be compared to the soul or heart image you drew in Step One when you began your healing journey. Let your creative spirit run wild and free as you create healing images that portray your heart's vision of your healed self, your grateful self, your healthy, vibrant self, and your sacred self. As you create these images, you can be confident in knowing that they are not just the fanciful tokens of an imagination let loose. They are, in fact, physio-neuro inducers that will activate a complete transformation of your body, mind, and spirit. As such, I encourage you to use these healing images as focal points for meditation in the coming weeks after you complete the program. Meditating on these images of yourself as fully healed will stimulate your autonomic nervous system to act on their autosuggestive messages.

Figure 72: *How My Soul Feels Now,* by Anne Mimi Sammis

"My soul no longer feels frightened and exposed. It is protected within the womb of the sacred mother—me. I am surrounded by the yellow light of empowerment and the loving energy of my heart. Within the protective and nurturing womb I hold the wounded child that was also me deep within my heart where it is being loved and healed."

EXERCISE ONE

Draw an Image of How Your Heart or Soul Feels Now

• Close your eyes and bring your awareness into your heart center. Ask your heart for an image that represents how it or your soul (whichever feels more comfortable) feels now that you have completed this healing work to integrate all aspects of your wounded, fragmented self into your life. When you know what that image is, draw it.

• When you have completed the drawing, go back and take out the first drawing you did in Step One of how your heart or soul was feeling when you began the program. Look at the two drawings and compare them. Notice how it feels to look at each drawing. Then answer the processing questions that follow.

Processing Questions

1. How did it feel to look at your first heart or soul drawing?

2. What are the differences between that first drawing and the one you just did? Any similarities?

3. How did it feel to do this second heart or soul drawing?

4. What do you imagine this second drawing is telling you about how your heart or soul is responding to the healing work you have done in this program?

5. What do the colors tell you about how your soul or heart feels now?

6. Are there any details in your drawing that might be trying to tell you something important about the way your heart or soul feels?

7. Is there anything about your drawing that confuses or disturbs you? If so, what?

8. What have you learned from this drawing about the healing that has taken place within you?

Figure 73: *The Healed Heart,*
by Anne Mimi Sammis

"This is a symbol of my healed heart, representing my pain transformed. I'm not alone anymore, in terror, being in the pain, the way I was when I began this work. I have now become the love I feel in my heart, and that allows me to look at the pain and not identify with it. I can see now that I have an absolute choice as to whether I want to go into the pain—to stay in my mind and relive it or if I want to go into my heart. My choice is to let go of the pain and stay in my heart."

EXERCISE TWO

Draw an Image of Yourself as Fully Healed in Body, Mind, and Spirit

Throughout this program you have been working on all the elements of the healing process, and the work you've done as you probed deeper into your pain has certainly been healing. However, the actual state of *being healed* is a separate occurrence. It is now time to transition from the process of healing into what is called the "end state" of being healed.

To enact the end state, you need to change your image associations to images that represent you as completely healed. In this exercise, you will ask your heart for an image that represents you as fully healed in body, mind, and spirit.

- With eyes closed and your attention focused on your body, move your awareness into your heart center and ask your heart for an image that represents you as fully healed in body, mind, and spirit.
- When you know what that image is, draw it.

Processing Questions

1. What did it feel like to draw this heart image of yourself as fully healed?

2. How does it feel to look at this image?

3. What does this image tell you about your heart's view of you as fully healed?

4. What do the colors tell you?

5. Are any details trying to tell you something important?

6. If this drawing could speak, what would it say?

7. What have you learned from this image?

Gratitude Closes the Door on Anger, Hatred, and Resentment

To keep anger, hatred, and resentment alive, you have to give these feelings a place to live. If you feed and harbor them, they will stay and grow. If you close the door on them, they will leave. Gratitude closes that door. If you take the time to be grateful for all that you are and all that you have—and hold those images in your heart and mind, anger, hatred, and resentment will wither and die. They simply cannot survive in an environment of gratitude.

The next exercise will help you envision an image of gratitude for yourself as healed. Hopefully you can see now what you couldn't see when you were totally immersed in your pain—the lessons your pain has taught you, the gifts it has given you. If you take anything with you from your experience with this program, I hope it is knowing that when the heart lies fallow in the darkened winter of our pain, faith and hope become the fertile ground of spring in which the beauty of life can bloom once again. Gratitude nurtures that fertile ground, keeping the blossoms of life alive and flourishing, no matter what hardships and obstacles we may face.

Figure 74: *Symbol of Gratitude,* by Anne Mimi Sammis

"This is my heart's symbol of gratitude. The two crosses embrace my heart. They symbolize my gratitude that Christ is there to help us heal. Love is embodied in the rainbow energy connecting the crosses, and a shaft of light moves through the middle, symbolizing protectiveness."

EXERCISE THREE

Draw a Symbol of Gratitude from Your Heart

- Get comfortable, close your eyes, and move your awareness into your heart center. Ask your heart for a symbol that represents its feeling of gratitude for all that you have learned in the healing process.
- When you know what that symbol is, draw it.

Processing Questions

1. How did it feel to draw this symbol?

2. How does it feel to look at it?

3. What is this symbol trying to tell you about your heart's feeling of gratitude?

4. What do the colors express about your heart's gratitude?

5. Are there any details that may be trying to tell you something about gratitude?

6. What have you learned about gratitude from this drawing?

Figure 75: *The Healing Spiral,* by Joya Peterson

"This drawing represents how it feels to be healed: alive, juicy, and unending. The drawing is a spiral of pure energy. It has movement and sound. It can change shape. Just looking at it activates me."

Your Healthy, Vibrant Self

What does being healthy and vibrant mean to you? How does that feel? To feel it, you must be able to see it as an image in your mind and body. Exercise Four will guide you to access your own inner image of what it feels like to be a healthy and vibrant you.

Occasionally, you may feel a sensation of expansive creativity overtake your sensibilities, especially when you're doing a feel-good, healing drawing. When that happens, you may want to allow yourself to go beyond the flat surface of your drawing paper by adding on more paper to build up or expand the drawing surface. You can cut or tear your paper or fold and shape it into a three-dimensional form. You can also incorporate some of those found objects I suggested collecting back in Chapter Four.

SOME EXAMPLES OF THREE-DIMENSIONAL AND COLLAGE DRAWINGS

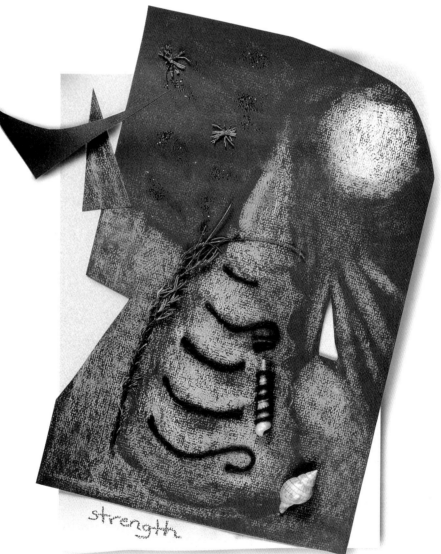

Figure 76: *Strength,*
by Mary Ellen Madsen

"The conical form comes up frequently for me. It's a symbol of healing because it represents my faith: a faith in myself that I will prevail through the difficult and painful upward journey I am going through. The string wrapped around the conical form and the shell represent the convoluted journey I am on— struggling to move upward on a path with many twists and turns, never knowing where I'm going or what the end will be like. This drawing/collage reaffirmed that I had the strength to continue that journey, even though I couldn't see an end in sight at the time."

93

Figure 77: *Heart and Soul,* by Barbara Ganim

"Feeling separated from my family roots with the loss of my parents, this drawing/collage tells me that the roots are still there, planted in the fertile soil of love. They have grown upward from the ground beneath the tree, through the tree, where they emerged at the top to form a new growth with its own roots. The dried fruit represents the fruits of my own growth—the growth of my heart and soul. Even though my parents are gone, what they gave me continues on, represented by the nest in the tree. The feathers and wing-like leaf forms symbolize taking flight on my own."

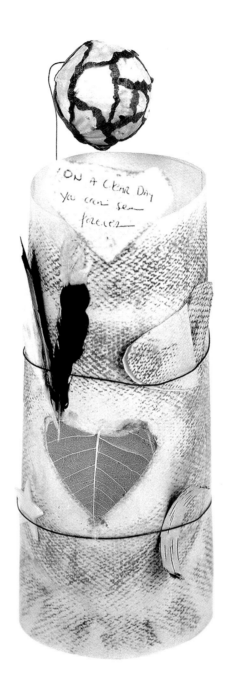

Figure 78: *On a Clear Day,* by Kina King

"The idea for the cylinder and the sphere—the ball on top—came to me during meditation, because it represents how nothing can cling to me. I am open to creative ideas, but they can flow into me through the cylinder. I drew a heart in the sphere, because I feel more focused on me now than when I first came into this group. I have given up focusing on all those other people who were renting space in my head. They were jabbering at me all the time. Now I've started a whole new career path. I couldn't do that before, because I couldn't focus. This form represents me as healed and healthy. I wrote, 'On a clear day,' on the heart, because those words represent how I can see clearly now."

EXERCISE FOUR

Draw an Image of Your Healthy, Vibrant Self

In this exercise, you will access your own inner image of what it feels like to be healthy and vibrant.

• Close your eyes and think about how good it is to feel well, to feel healthy, to feel vibrant. Then focus your attention on your body as you think about yourself as healthy and healed. Notice how your body responds to that thought. Imagine what feeling good, healthy, and vibrant would look like if it were an image.
• When you know what that image is, draw it.

Processing Questions

1. How did it feel to connect with your body's reaction to your thoughts about feeling good and healthy?

2. Where in your body did you feel this reaction?

3. What did it feel like to do this drawing?

4. How does it feel to look at it?

5. What does this drawing tell you about your body's reaction to feeling healthy and vibrant?

6. What do your colors tell you about feeling good?

7. If you used any found objects or expanded your drawing into a three-dimensional piece, how did that enhance your image?

8. If this drawing could speak, what would it say?

Transcending Your Pain

The final stage of the healing process occurs when we can transcend our pain. That doesn't mean ignoring it or disconnecting from it—it means moving beyond the pain, yet honoring what it has taught us. Transcendence allows our pain to become the source of our strength. You will know when you have fully transcended your pain when you can imagine an image of your spirit expanding and conjoining with its divine source of power—which could be God, the universe, your higher self, whatever you believe a divine power might be. The final exercise in this program is the culmination of your healing journey: creating an image of your sacred self.

Figure 79: *My Sacred Self,* by Jan

"This is an image of my sacred self—that part of me that is now healed and can move beyond pain and reach into the eternal. My sacred self sees life in full color instead of the darkness that has been with me for so long. It is passionate, yet its passion is controlled. That's important, because when I'm in pain I feel out of control. This image of me can move and dance. It has no boundaries. It cannot be contained."

EXERCISE FIVE

Draw an Image of Your Sacred Self

- Close your eyes and move your awareness into your heart center. Ask your heart for an image that represents your sacred self—that part of you that is divine and enlightened, that eternal part that can move beyond the physicality of your earthbound existence.
- When you know what that image of your sacred self would look like, draw it.

Processing Questions

1. What did it feel like to draw an image of your sacred self?

2. How does it feel to look at this image?

3. What does this image tell you about how your heart sees your sacred self?

4. What do the colors tell you about your sacred self?

5. Are any details in this drawing trying to tell you something more about your sacred self?

6. If you used any collage materials or created a three-dimensional form, how did that enhance your image?

7. If this image could speak, what would it say about your sacred self?

8. What have you learned about yourself from this image?

9. What have you learned about your pain from this program?

Meditating on Your Healing Images

The healing symbols or images you have created in this final step of the program will continue to activate you in body, mind, and spirit just by looking at them on a regular basis. The best way to stimulate their healing message and keep it alive within you is to spend a few minutes each day using one of the images—whichever one happens to suit your needs at the time—as a focal point for meditation.

How to Know If You Are Really Healed

How do you know if you are really healed? When you're in pain, it's hard to talk about it. To test whether or not you have healed the pain you've been working on, try talking with someone about it.

*like a branch bending in the wind . . .
at times ready to snap —
or able to swing back into position.*

— *Sabra*

Figure 80: *How Precarious Life Seems,* by Sabra Park

"Life is like a branch bending in the wind, at times ready to snap or able to swing back into position."

Figure 81: *A Soul's Journey,* by Theresa Walker

"I drew this flower image weeks after my mother's death when I felt grief and sadness. Once I had it down in my sketchbook I found it healing and consoling. In the days following its creation it would sometimes come into my mind spontaneously. To me the image says eternal life, rebirth, a soul's journey, a love that endures, the essence of who my mother is, and what she means to me."

Talking with a therapist is always best, but if you are feeling comfortable, then talk with a loved one or a trusted friend. Talk specifically about what was causing your pain, how you felt before you began this program, and how you feel now. If you can talk about your pain and the circumstances that provoked it without the pain resurfacing, then you are healed. It doesn't mean that you won't still feel something as you talk. That feeling may be sadness or even a sense of loss, but the overwhelming feeling of pain that you had before you began the program should be gone. If it isn't gone, fear not. That means you just need to give yourself more time. You may also need to do a little more drawing. Perhaps there is something more you haven't fully expressed yet. Keep working on it and be patient with yourself. Go back through the steps and see which ones call to you, imploring you to work with them again.

The Cure for Pain Is in the Pain

As I end this book, I am reminded of a quote by one of my favorite poets, Rumi, a thirteenth-century scholar, teacher, artist, and mystic from what is now Afghanistan. Rumi said, "The cure for pain is in the pain. Good and bad are mixed. If you don't have both, you don't belong with us." This quote brings me full circle, because I began the first chapter with a quote from one of my Drawing from the Heart support-group members, Phyllis Seelen, who said, "Pain isn't a bad thing . . . tears are a part of life . . . life will always be entwined with pain—you can't separate them." It is my hope that this program has brought you full circle in knowing that when difficult times weigh you down, drawing from the heart will make your pain much easier to bear.

Figure 82: *Wishful Thinking,* **by Julia Courtney**

"This very dark piece allowed me to explore the power of shame in my life. As a young adult I was very depressed. I made this drawing many years later when some old shame resurfaced. Making the image allowed me to keep the feelings in perspective and to know that they were just old feelings, and that they no longer had any power over me."

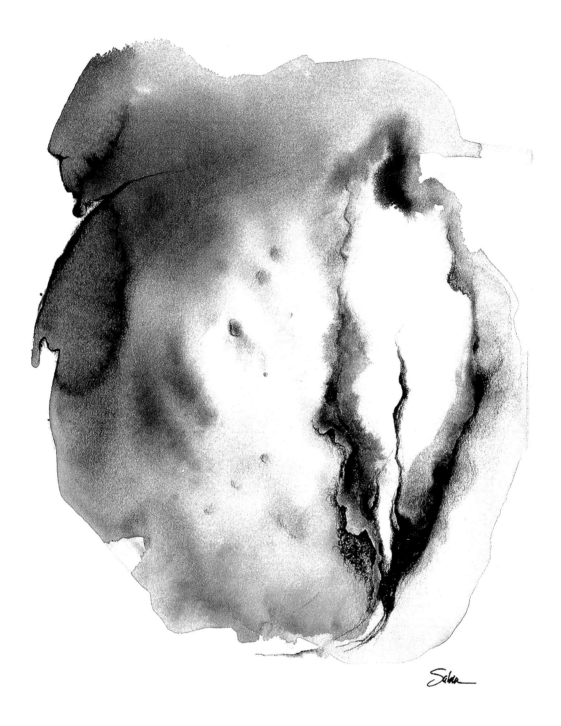

Figure 83: *View of Existence of the Soul,* by Sabra Park

*"This is that deep inner part of you that survives anything you might endure.
That part is true soul and it will heal from the inside out."*

About the Author

*B*arbara Ganim, M.A.E., C.H.H.C. is an expressive-arts educator, a certified holistic-health counselor, and an artist who specializes in the use of art, imagery, and visualization to help people with serious illness to heal. (She is an assistant professor of expressive arts and program coordinator at the Expressive Arts Institute at Salve Regina University in Newport, Rhode Island, in the University's Holistic Counseling Graduate Program. Barbara is also on the clinical staff of the Hope Center for Cancer Support in Providence, Rhode Island. She is also the author of *Art and Healing: Using Expressive Art to Heal Your Body, Mind and Spirit* (Crown/Three Rivers Press, 1999); coauthor with Susan Fox of *Visual Journaling: Going Deeper than Words* (Quest Books, 1999); and *The Healing Power of Art*, an audio-cassette program (Sounds True Productions, 2002). She lives in North Kingstown, Rhode Island.

If you wish to contact the author directly, you may write to:

Art as the Spirit of Healing
PO Box 1176
North Kingstown
Rhode Island 02852
or e-mail her at: Ganimb@Salve.edu

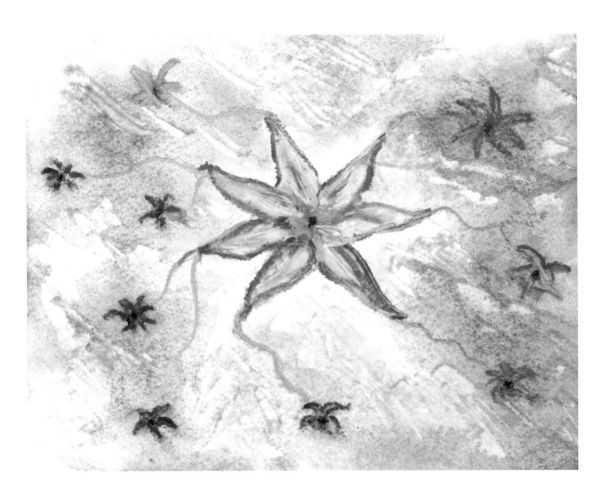

Being Supported, Birgitta Grimm

Additional Information on Expressive-Arts Degree and Nondegree Programs

*I*f you are interested in learning how to use expressive art for healing in psychotherapy, medical caregiving, or education, you may contact Barbara Ganim at Salve Regina University, 100 Ochre Point Avenue, Newport, Rhode Island 02840-4192; 401-847-6650, ext. 2157 for more information on any of the programs listed below:

The Expressive Arts Institute at Salve Regina University

Offers a three-weekend noncredit training program as an expressive-arts educational facilitator for professionals in the fields of psychotherapy, medical caregiving, education, business and industry, and the arts.

Graduate Certificate Program in the Expressive Arts at Salve Regina University

A program for those individuals with a Master's Degree who would like to specialize in the expressive arts and integrate them into their chosen profession. This program consists of fifteen graduate credits and is offered on weekends to accommodate distance learners. Prerequisite: The three-weekend expressive-arts training program.

Graduate Program in Holistic Counseling at Salve Regina University

The University offers a forty-eight-credit Master's Degree (M.A.) in Holistic Counseling, and a C.A.G.S. (Certificate of Advanced Graduate Study) in Expressive Art for those enrolled in the Master's Program in Holistic Counseling.